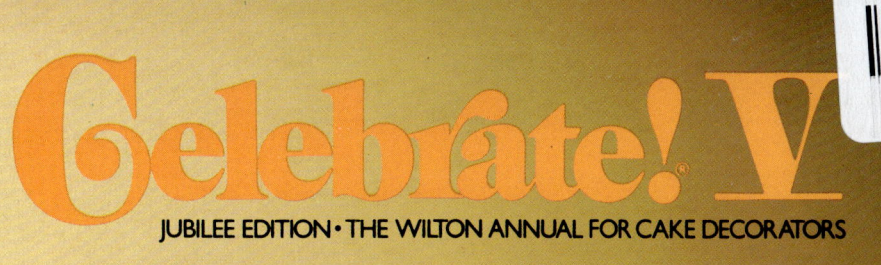

Celebrate! V

JUBILEE EDITION • THE WILTON ANNUAL FOR CAKE DECORATORS

EDITED BY EUGENE T. AND MARILYNN C. SULLIVAN

Jubilee! A cake for a golden anniversary or birthday. Decorating directions, page 144.

The brilliant cake on our cover is described on page 122.

A MESSAGE FROM THE PRESIDENT:
I'm especially proud to present this Jubilee issue of Celebrate!—it sums up a half century of both teaching an age-old art and of producing the quality products decorators need. We hope the 200 cakes and confections in this book will inspire you to create decorated pieces of your own. With the many Wilton products designed for homemakers to assist you, we know you can achieve the decorating triumphs everyone finds rewarding. Thanks to all of you who generously gave advice and shared experiences with us. You have helped us immeasurably.

VINCENT A. NACCARATO

Celebrate! V

DECORATING CONSULTANT: Norman Wilton
CO-EDITORS:
Marilynn C. Sullivan
and Eugene T. Sullivan
DECORATORS:
Michael Nitzsche, Senior decorator
Amy Rohr, Dong Tuy Hoa and
Dong Quy Nhung
ART ASSISTANT: Sandra Larson
EDITORIAL ASSISTANT: Melissa Jess
PRODUCTION ASSISTANT: Ethel LaRoche
READERS' EDITOR: Diane Kish
STAFF PHOTOGRAPHER: Edward Hois

Editorial mail should be addressed to:
  Wilton Book Division
  1603 South Michigan Avenue
  Chicago, Illinois 60616

Photographs and other material submitted for publication must be accompanied by a stamped, self-addressed envelope, if return is requested.

CELEBRATE!® V
THE ANNUAL FOR CAKE DECORATORS
is published by Wilton Enterprises, Inc.
2240 West 75th Street
Woodridge, Illinois 60515

Copyright © 1978 Wilton Enterprises, Inc.
All rights reserved. Reproduction in any way, without the prior written permission of the publisher, is expressly prohibited.

Library of Congress Catalog Card Number: 75-24148
International Standard Book Number: 0-912696-22-2

JUBILEE EDITION • THE WILTON ANNUAL FOR CAKE DECORATORS

The Sugar Plum Shop, 5

Fifty birthday cakes, each new as next week, fill this sunny new shop. Bright treasures for tots, girl's cakes with sweet personalities, swashbuckling cakes for boys. Brilliant cakes for teens, handsome action cakes to please a man and flowery creations to delight a lady! Each is an inspiration.

The Jubilee year

JANUARY/FEBRUARY, 39

Start the new year with fresh fruit and flower cakes, valentine cakes, ruffled and ribboned and trimmed with roses. Have fun with our Golden Oldies and winter frolic creations.

MARCH/APRIL, 55

Everything sings spring in this issue! A garden of flower cakes, pert bunnies, chirping chicks and a big egg cake tied with a bow! Meet two Irish gentlemen and learn how to figure pipe them. A bevy of pretty shower cakes.

MAY/JUNE, 71

Romance is in the air! A bouquet of beautiful bridal cakes, some reproduced from cakes trimmed decades ago. Delightful flowered cakes for Mother and real masterpieces to present to Dad. Two bright cakes for the graduate.

JULY/AUGUST, 95

All the pretty treats in this issue are decorated just for summer fun! See portable picnic cakes, red, white and blue cakes, animal treasures and water pleasures. Enjoy make-a-party cakes and nice new "thank you" cakes.

SEPTEMBER/OCTOBER, 109

School time! Bake bright new treats to send to class, have a halloween party and celebrate anniversaries with charming cakes of very unusual design. Learn three new flowers to pipe right on the cake.

NOVEMBER/DECEMBER, 123

Everything's planned for children in this issue—festive surprises to make this their happiest Christmas and provide treasured memories for holidays to come. Lots of cakes as cute as toys, new cookie treats, spectacular wreaths.

Good news for readers, 137

A parade of 28 prize-winning cakes in Celebrate's Jubilee Sheet Cake contest and the Sugar Plum Birthday Cake contest. These are the most imaginative cakes ever! 50 tips from our readers to make decorating easier and more fun. Readers' advice on decorating for profit and a few ways to prettier cakes from the *Celebrate!* staff.

Commonsense for cake decorators, 149

Down-to-earth advice from Norman Wilton on the uses of decorating tubes. Quick touches that give simple borders a professional look, lavish cake-side trims. A bouquet of flowers to pipe including the new Jubilee Rose. How to show off flowers to look their most beautiful on cakes.

Practical information for decorators, 158

How to cut party and wedding cakes. How many servings cakes of various sizes provide. All the tested icing recipes you'll need for cakes in this book.

INDEX, 160

OTHER WILTON BOOKS
The Wilton Way of Cake Decorating
   Volume One
The Wilton Way of Cake Decorating
   Volume Two
The Wilton Way of Cake Decorating
   Volume Three
Beautiful Bridal Cakes the Wilton Way
The Wilton Book of Wedding Cakes
Modern Cake Decorating
Discover the Fun of Cake Decorating
The Wilton Way to Decorate for Christmas
The Wilton Way of Making
   Gum Paste Flowers
Celebrate! Omnibus
Celebrate! II
Celebrate! III
Celebrate! IV
Celebrate! VI
The Complete Wilton Book of Candy
Celebrate! CHRISTMAS

Celebrate!® V

Third printing, July, 1982

Dear Friends,

For all of us, preparing this book has been pure enjoyment! Celebrate! V marks our Jubilee year—the 50th anniversary of Wilton Enterprises.

In 1929, my father, Dewey McKinley Wilton, founded Wilton Enterprises by starting the Wilton School of Decorating. By now, many thousands of students have graduated—some teach the Wilton Way themselves, others have found life-long pleasure in practicing this creative art form.

In 1952, we realized that we could reach many more people by giving them a book that would teach them decorating through picture lessons. That book was Modern Cake Decorating. Since it was first published, we've printed more than a half million copies. We've received thousands of letters and pictures from readers, telling us that they learned decorating from it, and later, from other Wilton books.

This first book created a need. In those days, cake decorating supplies were not available except to bakers, so we began to design and manufacture the things our readers needed and distribute them by mail. We still do. In addition, Wilton products are available in hundreds of shops and stores.

So it's really you who have built Wilton Enterprises—all of you who love decorating and love creating beautiful cakes for the joy of others. I only wish we could all get together for a great big party—but there are millions of us now, so Celebrate! V is our birthday party.

Scattered through Celebrate! V you'll find lots of little anecdotes that tell of some of our struggles and successes during this half century. I think you'll enjoy reading them, and I'm sure you'll love the four-times-fifty cakes we've made for you.

Norman Wilton
NORMAN WILTON

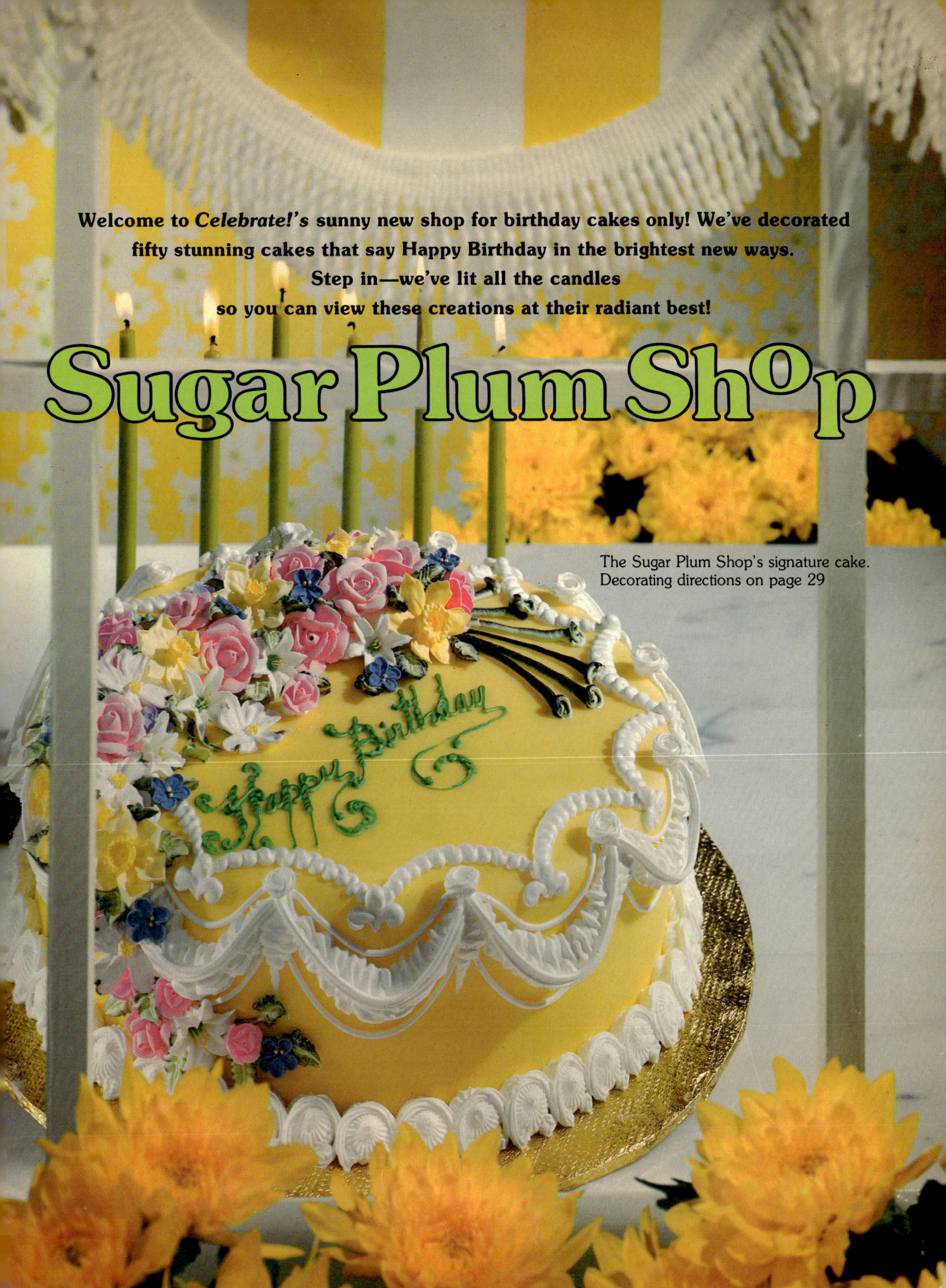

Welcome to *Celebrate!*'s sunny new shop for birthday cakes only! We've decorated fifty stunning cakes that say Happy Birthday in the brightest new ways. Step in—we've lit all the candles so you can view these creations at their radiant best!

Sugar Plum Shop

The Sugar Plum Shop's signature cake. Decorating directions on page 29

Quick & clever

Starting here is the most spectacular display of birthday cakes ever! Beginning with these cakes for the tiniest tots, you'll find many Quick & clever cakes and others more challenging to create for people of all ages.

Baby dolls for baby

Cute little baby dolls help to celebrate baby's first birthday.

1. The dolls begin with Small Wonder Mold cakes. Secure each to a cake base cut the same size as the cake. Ice cakes with a thin coat of buttercream. Cut a regular size marshmallow into fourths and use one piece for each foot. Press into icing. Mark scallops around base and pipe with a tube 3 line. Cover cakes with tube 14 stars.

2. For the head, insert a toothpick into a regular size marshmallow and dip into thinned royal icing. Insert toothpick into styrofoam block and dry.

3. Figure pipe arms with tube 8 and cover with tube 14 stars. Pipe hands with tube 8 and add tube 102 ruffles. Pipe tube 103 ruffle, following scallops at base of cake.

4. Insert toothpick on head into top of cake. Pipe hair and features with tube 2, cheeks with tube 3. Pipe tube 103 ruffle around face for front of bonnet and add a bow with same tube. Cover back of bonnet with tube 14 stars. Each little darling serves one. Set them on a sheet cake to serve a crowd!

A ship, lollipop trimmed

The sweetest toy ship sails into a tot's birthday celebration!

1. Bake 4″ high cake in the Long Loaf pan. Cut out the ship and cabin as shown in the diagram below. Ice ship and place on cake board, then ice the cabin and place it on top.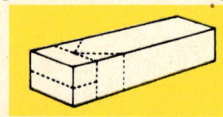

2. Swirl blue and white icing together so the colors are not completely mixed. Pipe the waves with tube 22 comma shapes, then add tube 16 elongated shells on cake board between them. Mark a line 1″ below top edge of ship. Pipe tube 16 stars to fill area between line and top edge of cake. Secure mint portholes with icing to side of ship.

3. Wrap a fat 4″ tall candle with ribbon, gluing it in place. Secure candle to top of cabin. Pipe tube 16 blue stars on top of cabin, white stars around base of cabin. Push candles in clear holders and lollipops into top of ship. Cut paper pennant and glue to florists' wire. Pipe tube 2 lettering, then insert wire into cake. This good ship serves about 14.

Roll in a pull toy

Recreate a child's pull toy, a cart filled with blocks. Trimmed with shining gelatin shapes, it's quick to make, fun to eat and easy to serve.

1. Make ¼″ thick gelatin trims using the recipe on page 128. Use oiled daisy and alphabet cutters for cutting the gelatin flowers and name.

2. Bake and ice a 9″ x 13″ x 2″ single-layer sheet cake. Attach cake to a 9″ x 13″ cake base. Secure a 1″ thick, 4½″ x 6½″ piece of styrofoam to a 12″ x 15½″ foil-covered board, then attach cake on top. Divide cake into sixths on the long sides, fourths on the short sides. Mark lines across top of cake, connecting the divisions, with a piece of light cardboard. Pipe over the marked lines with tube 14. Cover the sides of the cake with tube 15 stars.

3. Secure doughnut wheels to sides of cake with icing, then attach a mint and life saver to each one. Make pull cord of ribbon and life savers and attach with icing. Trim cake top with gelatin trims and candles in clear holders. Serve to twelve guests.

Tot's treasures

Candy and cookies and everything cute trim these bright cakes for the pre-school set. His birthday is the biggest day of the year for a little child—so decorate the cake with lots of love.

Favorite TV friends

Ask the whole Sesame Street* gang to the party to show what fun it is to be five. (Three and four are enjoyable ages too!)

1. Prepare the cookies first. Use the Sesame Street Cookie Cutter set, a number cutter and this recipe, or your own favorite.

ROLL-OUT COOKIES
- 1¼ cups butter
- 2 cups sugar
- 2 eggs
- 5 cups flour
- 2 teaspoons baking powder
- 1 teaspoon salt
- ½ cup milk
- ¼ teaspoon grated orange peel

Cream butter and sugar together, then add eggs and beat until fluffy. Sift dry ingredients together and add alternately to creamed mixture with milk. If mixture is too sticky, add a little more flour so that it is easy to handle. Roll dough ¼" thick and cut. Lift cookies with large spatula and place on ungreased cookie sheet.

Bake in 375°F oven eight minutes or until edges are light golden brown. This makes about four dozen large cookies.

After cookies have cooled, tint royal icing for trim. With tube 2, outline cookies 1/16" in from edge and around color areas, following indentations on cookies. Thin the icing and flow in the areas. After icing has dried, add final touches with tube 2.

2. Bake a two-layer 10" square tier and a 6" single-layer square tier. Place 6" tier on cake base and ice. Fill 10" tier, set on cake base. Lightly mark two curves on side of tier. Ice top and area within curves white, remainder of sides yellow. Assemble tiers.

3. Pipe birthday wishes with tube 2. Do star border at base of cake with tube 20, remaining borders with tube 17. Trim with tube 3 red dots. Push in tall tapers. Now attach the cookies on mounds of icing, propping with toothpicks as needed. Light the candles and serve to 23 little guests.

Spell it with lollipops

Here's a very sweet way to say "Happy Birthday" to a little boy or girl.

1. Bake, fill and ice two-layer tiers—10" and 6" round. Insert ¼" dowels, clipped off level with surface, in 10" tier to support tier above. Assemble on cake board or serving tray.

2. Pipe tubes 33 and 190 drop flowers in royal icing. Add tube 2 centers and dry. Print letters on lollipops with tube 3. Pipe curved base border on 10" tier with tube 19, top border with tube 17. Pipe tube 17 base shell border on 6" tier, drop tube 13 strings from top edge and finish with tube 16 top shell border. Pipe a curving vine around side of 10" tier with tube 4, trim with tube 66 leaves and attach flowers on dots of icing.

3. Place drop flowers on top of tiers, push in lollipops and candles and sing the birthday song! Serves 20.

Everybody's smiling . . .

because it's a party! Cookie portraits of each guest march around the sides of the birthday cake.

1. Bake and trim the cookies first, the rest of the decorating will go quickly. Use your favorite recipe, or the one above and cut out as many cookies as there are guests with the Giant Girl cutter. Trim off skirt for boy figures. Cut seven or eight 2¼" round "balloon" cookies and lay on damp popsicle sticks to bake.

When cookies have cooled, outline balloons with tube 2 and royal icing. Fill in with thinned icing and paint popsicle sticks. Outline clothing areas of people cookies and fill in with thinned icing. Dry, then add tube 2 features, hair and details. Do lettering on balloons with same tube.

2. Bake and ice a Long Loaf cake. Pipe bulb border at base with tube 12, top border with tube 9. Push appropriate number of candles into top of cake. Attach people cookies on sides with mound of icing, propping with bits of toothpicks as needed. Insert balloon cookies on top of cake above "people." Set this creation on the party table and receive applause! Serves 16.

*© 1977 Children's Television Workshop BIG BIRD, COOKIE MONSTER, THE COUNT, ERNIE, BERT, OSCAR THE GROUCH © 1971, 1973, 1977 Muppets Inc.

Quick & clever

The youngsters will love these four fast, fabulous cakes. They're just as much fun as a circus! Descriptions begin at upper left and move clockwise.

Four clowns in a row

Jolly, roly-poly clowns on this happy cake set the festive mood of the party.

1. Make the clowns first. Bake cupcakes, allowing tops to mound up. Insert a toothpick into each of four marshmallows, then dip them in thinned royal icing and dry. Swirl icing on cupcakes for round effect. Pipe tube 12 arms on each, then tube 8 hands. Pipe neck ruffle with tube 8, then insert the toothpicks on the marshmallow heads down into the cupcakes. Add hair, eyes, nose, mouth and buttons with tube 5, then hat with tube 2B and place a miniature marshmallow on top of hat.

2. Bake a 4" high cake in the Long Loaf pan. Ice and place on cake board. Use miniature marshmallows placed next to each other for the base border. Push them into the icing on the side of the cake to keep them in position. Place clowns on top of cake. Pipe legs with tube 2A, shoes with tube 8. Insert slim tapers into cake top behind clowns. Add a card with tube 2 message and a ribbon bow. Each clown serves one, loaf cake serves 16.

Three-ring circus

Treat the birthday child to the excitement of a three-ring circus! Cute novelty figures provide the action.

1. Bake a 9" x 13" two-layer sheet cake, a 5" x 3" round, two-layer cake and two 5" x 1½" round, single-layer cakes. Fill and ice the two-layer cakes, ice the single-layer cakes. Place sheet cake on serving tray and position the 5" two-layer cake on top to the rear. Trim 5" cake with a tube 48 curved line on the side and add a red candy within each curve, securing with a dot of icing. Pipe tube 6 ball borders.

2. Divide the side of each 5" single-layer cake into twelfths. On one, pipe vertical tube 48 stripes at each division; on the other, pipe diagonal tube 48 stripes. Place the single-layer cakes on top of sheet cake toward the front. Pipe tube 6 ball borders on each.

3. Pipe message on side of sheet cake with tube 6. Add bottom ball border with tube 10. Place Ball-Balancing Seal, Performing Lion and Lion Tamer figures on top of the 5" cakes. Insert slim tapers near the back of the sheet cake. To serve, cut the 5" single-layer cakes in half, the 5" two-layer cake into four pieces and the sheet cake into 24 for a total of 32 servings.

Happy faces

The smiling clown faces on this bright birthday cake are so easy to make that they take almost no time at all!

1. Bake, fill and ice an 8" square, two-layer cake. Place on a serving tray or cake board. On each side of cake, use a 2" round cookie cutter as a pattern press for the faces. Using tube 16, pipe face outline, hat, hair, ears and neck ruffle. Pipe the facial features and ball on hat with tube 6.

2. Pipe base and top shell border with tube 16. Add lettering on cake top with tube 3, then insert slim tapers into cake. Serve to twelve happy guests.

Sweet clown trio

Topped with a trio of sugar mold clowns, this cute cake is quick to make and lots of fun for the birthday child.

1. Mold six clowns using Circus Molds set and the sugar mold recipe and technique described below.

SUGAR MOLD RECIPE
  2½ pounds granulated sugar
  1 egg white

Stir egg white lightly with a fork, then mix with sugar. Knead mixture with hands about one minute. To tint, substitute liquid food color for the same amount of egg white and blend in by hand. Pack sugar into mold as firmly as possible. If making more than four with the same mold, dust mold with cornstarch to prevent sticking. Scrape off excess sugar mixture with spatula so top is perfectly flat and level with edge of mold. Unmold at once. Place piece of cardboard over mold, turn upside down, lift mold off. Shape dries hard in about five hours (longer in humid weather). Or place in 200°F oven for five minutes.

2. With royal icing, attach two clowns together, back to back, with toothpicks extending from legs to form a 3-D figure. Paint colored areas with thinned royal icing. Dry, then pipe eyes and mouth with tube 3, nose with tube 5.

3. Bake and fill a 10" round, two-layer cake. Swirl on icing, and place on a serving tray. Pipe tube 18 rosette base border. Add message with tube 3. Push toothpicks on clowns into top of cake. Insert a candle behind each clown and serve to ten little birthday party guests.

Sugar Plum Shop

Thrill a little girl with a once-in-a-lifetime, one-of-a-kind birthday cake

Look at me! I'm seven

Any little girl from six to ten will be speechless with delight when she sees this amazing cake. There she stands in her best party dress and new shoes seeing her pretty image in a mirror! This bit of magic is achieved by creating two identical gum paste figures with a mirror frame between them. The little cake-top tableau can be lifted off before serving. She'll save it as a treasured memento of an exciting birthday.

1. Do figures and mirror in advance. Make a recipe of gum paste (below) and tint small portions. Mold and dress two identical figures in the five-year-old child molds from the People Mold set. Follow directions that accompany the molds. When positioning the figures, bend opposite arms so they will create a mirror effect. Be sure to copy the dress and hair-do the little birthday girl will be wearing to her party.

2. Cut mirror frame from gold gum paste using *Celebrate! V* pattern. Cut a 5½" circle for base of tableau. Dry flat. Mold two Mantle designs from Baroque molds set. Cut in half vertically for legs of mirror. Save top center part for top trim. Dry legs with lower part of design propped ¼" higher than upper part.

3. Attach top center piece and legs to mirror frame. Attach any two pieces of dried gum paste by brushing a tiny piece of wet gum paste with egg white, placing on first piece, brushing again and adding second piece. Use matching royal icing to trim mirror. Pipe a tube 4 line down the center with royal icing. On outer edge, pipe tube 13 shells, on inner edge pipe tube 4 beading. Dry, then turn over and pipe back the same as front. Attach small balls of gum paste under the outer part of the legs. Attach mirror in center of gum paste circle, then attach girl's figures on either side of mirror. Spray twice with clear acrylic spray.

4. Pipe drop flowers with tubes 225, 131 and 33. Add tube 2 centers.

Bake, fill and ice a 10" round, two-layer cake. Place on cake board. Pipe tube 20 comma shapes around base of cake. Divide side of cake into eighths and drop a string guideline from point to point. Insert Push-In candle holders. Pipe tube 16 top shell border. Attach drop flowers with dots of icing along guidelines. Trim with tube 66 leaves.

5. Cut a 5½" circle of clear plastic and place in center of cake top, then set tableau on plastic. Edge with tube 4 beading. Insert candles. Serves 14.

GUM PASTE

- 1 tablespoon Gum-tex™ or tragacanth gum
- 1 heaping tablespoon glucose
- 3 tablespoons warm water
- 1 pound confectioners' sugar (or more)

Mix Gum-tex™ and glucose until smooth and dissolved. Add warm water, one tablespoon at a time. Stir in small amounts of confectioners' sugar until you can work mixture with your hands. Continue adding small amounts of sugar as you knead until you have added about ¾ pound of sugar. Gum paste handles best when aged, so store in a plastic bag at least overnight, then break off a piece and work in more sugar until pliable but not sticky. Always keep portion you are not working with well-covered. To color, knead in a little paste food color. For flat pieces, roll a small piece on a cornstarch-dusted surface and cut.

Daisy patch, Quick & clever

The quickest, sweetest cake ever!

1. Bake an 8" square, two-layer cake. Fill, ice and place on serving tray. On each side, use flower cutter from Four-Season cookie cutter set as a pattern press. Pipe shell petals and leaves with tube 20, stems and rosette centers with tube 16. Fill bottom border between the flowers with tube 16 stars.

2. Pipe tube 16 top shell border, then pipe "C"-shaped curves on top of cake with the same tube. Print tube 2 greeting and insert slim tapers. Serve to twelve party guests.

Big beautiful

dolls...

Queen of the day

A very pretty doll in a flowered party dress is surrounded by bow-tied "present" cakes. You might use this idea for a sweet sixteen celebration.

1. Cut the presents from a sheet cake, 2" high. Chill the cake, then cut it into 2" squares. Ice each cube with white buttercream, then cover with Quick Poured Fondant (page 159). After fondant sets, pipe ribbons with tube 44 and add tube 101 bows. Insert a candle in a clear holder in each present.

2. Bake and decorate the doll. Pipe tube 23 drop flowers with tube 2 centers and dry. Bake a cake in a Large Wonder Mold, chill and attach to cardboard cake circle. Ice thinly and insert Little Girl doll pick. Mound icing at top of cake to meet waistline of doll. Set on pedestal cake stand.

Drop three rows of tube 2 string to define curved ruffles on skirt. Starting at base, pipe tube 14 stars up to string guidelines. Pipe tube 101 ruffles on skirt, following guidelines, then continue covering skirt with stars and ruffles. Cover bodice area with stars, over-piping at shoulder for puffed sleeves. Edge sleeves with a tube 101s ruffle. Circle neckline with flowers, attaching with dots of icing, and sprinkle more flowers over dress.

3. Set doll cake, on pedestal, in center of large round tray or cake board and circle with present cakes. Serve each guest a present—doll serves twelve.

Garden girls

One of the cutest cakes you could bake for a little girl, and surprisingly easy.

1. Pipe tube 225 drop flowers with tube 2 centers in royal icing. Dry. Thread a marshmallow, then a miniature marshmallow, then a second marshmallow on a toothpick. This forms head, neck and bodice. Make eight of these, then dip in thinned flesh-colored icing and set in styrofoam block to dry.

2. Bake a two-layer 8" square cake and four Small Wonder Mold cakes. Chill all the cakes, ice Wonder Molds thinly, then cut each in half. Fill and ice the square cake and pat with a damp sponge. Set in center of a 14" cake board and press two half-Wonder Mold

Continued on page 38

He'll always remember the birthday you trimmed one of these brilliant cakes!

Sand castle, Quick & clever

There's never been a boy who didn't love to build castles on the beach. Build him one for his birthday—it's easier than building it in sand!

1. The castle is formed of a 10″ square, two-layer cake, two cakes baked in Small Wonder Molds, four in 6-ounce frozen orange juice cans, and a single-layer 6″ round cake. Fill the square cake, measure 1″ in from each corner, cut off corners and ice. Pat with damp sponge for sandy surface. Set on cake board. Trim off edges of cakes baked in juice cans, ice and set against corners of square cake. Pat with damp sponge. Ice and "stucco" the other cakes and cones and assemble as picture shows.

2. Pipe tube 7 bulb borders on upper cakes and a tube 8 border on square cake. Glue paper banners, about 4″ long, to lengths of stiff florists' wire. Pipe lettering with tube 1 and stick banners into towers. Top each wonder mold cake with a tall taper and add more candles set in clear holders. An architectural gem that serves about 29.

Knighthood is in flower

Here's a cake with all the color and adventure of the glorious days of chivalry! The knights are done in Color Flow on gum paste for added strength. When the party's over, they're handsome enough to frame.

1. Do the six knights first using *Celebrate! V* patterns. Roll out tinted gum paste (recipe page 13) and cut out along outlines of figures with a sharp knife. Dry about 24 hours, then trace details of figures on shapes. Outline with tube 1 and flow in thinned icing. When knights are dry, add features with tube 1. Paint a 10″ dowel rod with thinned icing. Cut a paper banner about 2½″ square and pipe trim and name with tube 1. Glue to dowel rod.

2. Bake, fill and ice yellow a 12″ two-layer round tier and a 6″ two-layer hexagon tier. Insert dowel rods, clipped level with top into round cake for support. Assemble the tiers. Mark center of top of hexagon tier and connect with each corner. Fill in each panel with tube 15 stars, starting at bottom and continuing across top to center mark. Use vivid red, green and blue icing.

3. Transfer "Happy Birthday" pattern to cake side and pipe with tube 13. Add a fleur-de-lis between each word. Divide side of cake into twelfths near base, and pipe a tube 17 fleur-de-lis at each division. Do bottom shell border with tube 18. Pipe twelve tube 17 fleurs-de-lis on top of cake and finish top border with tube 17 shells.

4. Stand knights around the hexagon tier, securing with mounds of icing. Insert tall tapers in hexagon tier and smaller candles in clear holders in round tier. Set in the banner and add a tube 13 twirl. Watch the boys' eyes shine when you bring in the cake! Serves 28.

It's a boy's world

18

Bake him a lively birthday cake as full of fun as he is

Sails in the breeze
Quick & clever

A creek, a pond, even a mud puddle brings out the sailor in a boy. Launch these boats on an icing lake!

1. Make boats from gingerbread. Roll out about ⅜" thick and cut using *Celebrate! V* pattern. Cut holes for candles using tubes 2A and 12. Bake and cool.

GINGERBREAD
    5 to 5½ cups all-purpose flour
    1 teaspoon baking soda
    1 teaspoon salt
    2 teaspoons ginger
    2 teaspoons cinnamon
    1 teaspoon nutmeg
    1 teaspoon cloves
    1 cup shortening
    1 cup sugar
    1¼ cups unsulphured molasses
    2 eggs, beaten

Thoroughly mix flour, soda, salt and spices. Melt shortening in large saucepan. Add sugar, molasses and eggs; mix well. Cool slightly, then add four cups of the dry ingredients and mix well. Turn mixture onto lightly floured surface. Knead in remaining dry ingredients by hand. Roll out and cut pieces. Place on greased cookie sheet with spatula. Bake at 375°F for eight to ten minutes until done. Let cool on cookie sheet a few minutes, remove and cool completely on rack.

2. Bake, fill and ice with boiled icing, a 12" x 4" round, two-layer cake. Swirl icing on top. Place on serving tray. Place boats on top, pressing them into icing. Pipe tube 20 bottom shell border, tube 18 top shell border. Trim side of cake with tube 16 colonial scrolls. Insert tall thin taper at front of boats, small candle at back. Cut 3" x 5" sails from light cardboard. (Use index cards.) Punch a hole ⅜" from each end. Slip sails over tall tapers, then pipe tube 1 message. Serves 22 sailors.

Soap box derby
Quick & clever

Wave the checkered flag for your winner on his birthday!

1. Bake four 2½" round cookies for wheels and half of a 2" cookie for steering wheel. Use the gingerbread recipe above, or any firm cookie dough. Tape patterns for two rectangular and one star plaque to flat surface, cover with wax paper and outline with tube 2. Flow in Color Flow icing. Outline and flow in icing on cookies too. Dry, then add tube 1 writing to plaques.

2. Bake a 4" high cake in Long Loaf pan. At each end, measure in 4¼" and trim so ends taper to a point. Measure an area 3½" long for cockpit and carve down ½" deep. Secure to cake base cut same size and shape as cake. Attach a 2½" x 9½" piece of 1" thick styrofoam to a 17" x 6½" foil-covered cake board with icing, then secure cake on top.

3. Push two 5½" long dowel rods through sides of cake as axles. Attach plaques with icing, then cover car with tube 16 stars. Push steering wheel into icing in cockpit and attach wheels to axles with icing. Serves twelve.

His private hideaway

Every boy would love a tree house, so build one on his birthday cake!

1. Bake 12" x 4" round and 5" x 4" square, two-layer cakes. Fill between layers. Place each on a cake base the same size as cake. Ice 12" cake and place on tray.

2. Trim top of 5" cake on an angle to 3" height at back. Use thick and thin pretzels for roof and siding. Ice, then press pretzels into icing. Cut pretzels to length with a sharp knife. Pipe door knob with tube 5. Pipe face with tube 1 on candy wafer and secure in window. Make flag from paper and florists' wire, then pipe skull and crossbones with tube 1.

3. Pipe tube 22 tree trunk on side of 12" cake, extending up onto top. Push pretzel ladder rungs into icing. Add tube 15 branches. Place tree house in center of cake. Pipe tube 69 leaves. Circle base of cake with tube 6 bulb border, add grass with tube 233. Add Push-In holders and light the candles. Serve to 22 guests. The birthday boy gets the tree house.

Quick & clever treats for teens

Treat a teen to a bouquet blooming on a birthday cake! Bold colors and new and unusual techniques make the decorating easy, the effects spectacular. Watch the smiles, hear the ooh's and ah's of delight when you present your brilliant masterpiece!

Sunshine flowers

One of the most talked-about cakes in the Sugar Plum Shop! The radiant flowers are made of cookie dough, the "stained glass" centers are hard candy, baked right along with the cookies.

1. Use the cookie recipe on page 8, and tint small portions orange and yellow by kneading in liquid food color. Keep remainder of dough tightly wrapped in plastic. Line a cookie sheet with foil, shiny side up, and coat well with cooking oil (not solid shortening). Lay dampened popsicle sticks on the foil. Cut out flowers with the Giant Flower cutter and place the flower shapes on the sheet, most of the popsicle sticks extending. Cut out centers with a 2¼" round cutter (bake these separately). Lay three sour balls or four life savers in the open center of each flower and bake at 375°F for about eight minutes. Candy will have melted into transparent color! Cool until candy hardens, then carefully peel off foil. These cookies are so cute you might want to bake more to give to the guests.

2. Bake a two-layer 9" x 13" sheet cake. Chill layers, set on cardboard cake base and fill. Ice top with green buttercream and pat with damp sponge. Ice sides smoothly with white icing. Print greeting with tube 3 and pipe base comma-shaped border with tube 20, top shell border with tube 16. Paint the flower "stems" with thinned icing, dry and push flowers into cake. Add tube 68 leaves. Frame the garden with candles, set in Push-in holders. Serves 24.

Great big blossoms

Four fantastic, far-out flowers glow on a sheet cake! It's easy as 1-2-3!

1. Bake four cakes in Blossom pans, chill and set each on a cardboard cake base, cut to size and shape. Bake a two-layer 9" x 13" sheet cake, chill, fill and ice on a cake base. Transfer to serving tray.

2. Pipe message with tube 1 at center front of sheet cake. Cover blossom cakes with tube 125 curving petals, starting at base. Add tube 16 stars at top.

3. Arrange flowers on top of sheet cake and pipe tube 16 stems. Add long leaves with same tube. Finish with tube 16 rosettes at base of cake, tube 16 shell border at top. Set a tall taper in each flower and birthday candles in Push-in holders at sides of cake. Sheet cake serves 24, each flower two guests.

A new crazy daisy!

Just one big beautiful flower—that's this treat from the Sugar Plum Shop.

1. Bake a two-layer cake in 12" petal pans, chill, place on cardboard cake base, then fill and ice. Transfer to serving tray or cake board.

2. Lightly mark a 5" circle on top of cake. Pipe the big petals with tube 6B. In center of each curve of cake top, pipe a giant shell from edge to marked circle. Add a shell on each side. Now add a second series of eight shorter shell petals, using indentations of cake shape as guide. Fill center circle with a spiral piped with tube 32.

Add tube 13 string drapes and rosettes on cake sides and finish with a tube 18 shell border at base. Set candles in center. This big daisy serves 26 guests.

Space Cakes

Step into the Sugar Plum Shop and view our space cakes—they'll star at the best birthday parties of the year. We decorated them for teenagers, but any age will find them just as much fun. For a really fantastic celebration, you might want to do them all!

Space craft
Quick & clever

It's easy to float this far-out cake!
1. Just bake two cakes in 14" base bevel pans, and another only 1" high in a 6" round pan. Use a firm pound cake recipe and chill or freeze the cakes after baking. Set one bevel cake face down and ice the slant surface in blue sky icing. Turn upright on serving tray, ice the top and set the other bevel cake on it. Fasten with toothpicks, and ice the upper cake in wild green. Ice the 6" cake in ultra violet and set on top.
2. Now pipe tube 3 beading on all edges. Attach mints and life savers with icing for portholes. Make paper banners, pipe birthday message with tube 2, and glue them to a tall candle. Push candle into cake and add more candles in clear holders. Time for the birthday song! This craft serves about 14, depending on appetites.

Space people
Quick & clever

A vivid imagination, a few shaped pans and some candies are the main ingredients needed to bring this friendly little group to a birthday party.

1. Bake a 9" x 13" two-layer sheet cake, fill, ice and set on cake board. Pipe tube 18 rosette base border, print message with tube 14, and do top shell border with tube 16.
2. Now for the space people! You'll have lots of ideas of your own—here's how we baked the ones in the picture:
   Two Small Wonder Molds, small ends trimmed and put together, half of a Little Loafer for head.
   A Little Loafer, 2" circle of cake for head, marshmallow arms.
   Egg cupcakes, bases flattened.
   The other half of the Little Loafer.
   Two heart cupcakes iced together.
3. Ice all these shapes in wild colors, put together with toothpicks, edge with tube 2 and attach bright candies for features and trim. Make a cosy grouping of space people on the sheet cake, insert a candle in a clear holder in the head of each and start the party! Base cake serves 24, the guests will beg to take their space friends home.

Far planet
Quick & clever

Yes, you can create this planet to whirl into the birthday party. Shape it of round pans and a ball pan.

1. Bake round tiers just 1" high in 12", 10" and 8" pans. Bake a cake in the Ball pan. Chill the tiers, then carefully cut a 6" circle from the 8" tier. (This will be "one to go on".) Attach the 8" ring to a cake circle cut the same. Flatten the base of the ball cake and attach it to a 4" cake circle.
2. Ice all the tiers, the ball cake and the 6" circle. Put 10" tier atop 12" tier and insert dowel rods to support the ball. Set 8" ring on cake and lift back with a stack of sugar cubes iced together. Carefully set ball cake in ring, then pipe tube 3 bulb borders. Glue a paper pennant to a toothpick, pipe tube 2 lettering and stick into planet. Add birthday candles and set a tall candle in the 6" circle. The planet serves 12, rest of the cake about ten and the 6" circle belongs to the birthday child.

Rousing cakes for teens' birthdays from the Sugar Plum Shop

Bright colors, lots of action and generous size add up to outstanding cakes for teens' birthdays.

A trophy for a champ
The teams charge down the field to bring birthday wishes to the champ! The long loaf cake is so easy to cut and serve, you'll use the pan often.

1. Make Color Flow figures in advance. Tape *Celebrate! V* patterns to a flat surface and tape wax paper over. Outline with tube 1, then flow in thinned icing. Dry. Outline and flow in the numbers on the helmets and jerseys. Dry.

Paint a Vase and Pedestal Pillar with thinned royal icing for trophy. Dry, then do lettering on side with tube 1.

2. Bake a 4" high cake in the Long Loaf pan. Ice and place on a foil-covered cake board. Secure football players to side of cake with icing. Pipe tube 6 bottom ball border, then add tube 233 grass. Pipe tube 8 top ball border. Attach trophy to cake top with icing. Print "Happy Birthday" with tube 3 on cake top. Add candles in Push-In holders on sides of cake, Crystal Clear holders on top. Light the candles and serve to 16.

Let's hear it for a birthday!
Pompon girls lead the cheers on this exciting cake for a teen.

1. Make Color Flow figures in advance using *Celebrate! V* patterns. Outline with tube 1 and flow in thinned icing. Dry thoroughly, then pipe hair, eyes and mouths with tube 1. Dry.

2. Bake a 4" high Long Loaf cake. Ice, then place on a foil-covered cake board. Pipe tube 8 bottom bulb border, tube 6 bulb border at top and down corners. Secure pompon girls to cake with icing, attaching the two on either side first, then the middle one.

3. Insert three tall tapers into cake at one end and surround with pompons. Do this right on the cake. Pipe a tube 6 ball for base, then cover it with tube 233, starting at top of ball and working down. Pipe more pompons at ends of girls' arms. Add more candles in Push-In holders. Cuts into 16 servings.

A top 40 hit!
This sparkling cake sets the theme of the party—golden hits provide the sound effects. Every teen will love it!

1. Make the records very quickly from gum paste. Make a recipe of gum paste (page 13). Tint portions gold, green, red and orange. Roll out gold gum paste as thin as possible. Cut 14 records with a 3" round cutter and lay on a flat surface. Cut centers for records from the other colors with a 1⅜" cutter. Attach to the records with egg white, then cut a hole in the center of three records for the cake top with tube 12. Cut holes in remaining records with tube 10. Dry.

2. Make musical notes from gum paste rolled very thin. Cut bottom of note with Small Violet Leaf cutter from the Flower Garden Set, staff and top freehand. Assemble with egg white and dry on a flat surface.

3. Bake a 9" x 13" x 4" two-layer sheet cake, an oval single-layer tier 2" high and a 5" x 1½" round, single-layer tier, using Mini-tier pan. Fill the sheet cake, ice and place on a foil-covered cake board. Insert dowel rods, clipped level with surface, to support the upper tiers. Ice the single-layer tiers and stack them on top of the sheet cake. Pipe ball borders on all tiers, using tube 7 on the sheet cake, tube 5 on the oval and tube 4 on the round tier. Pipe tube 1 message on three records. Secure the three records with tube 12 holes on round tier with icing, then attach remaining records and notes to cake as picture shows. Insert tall, thin tapers into records on top of round tier. Add candles in Push-In holders on the sides of the sheet cake. Serves 34.

Pool table! *Quick & clever*

It's fun, it's fast, it's sure to please the man who enjoys playing pool.

1. Paint two 7″ dowel rods with thinned royal icing for cues. Using *Celebrate! V* pattern for rack, pipe, then over-pipe with tube 8 and royal icing on wax paper. Dry. Make Color Flow plaque using pattern and outlining with tube 2. Dry, then pipe tube 2 message.

2. Bake, fill and ice a 9″ x 13″ two-layer sheet cake. Make ridges on side with decorating comb. Place on cake board. Make depressions in top for pockets with a teaspoon, 1″ in from edge of cake. Pipe tube 16 base shell border. Pipe tube 17 zigzag around top of cake, then add tube 14 zigzag.

3. Secure plaque to side of cake. Add a few tube 26 drop flowers and tube 66 leaves. Place rack, cues and gum balls on cake top. Insert Push-In holders in side of cake and serve to 24.

Show a bachelor you care
Quick & clever

True blue flowers are the trim.

1. Pipe 20 royal icing bachelor buttons. Bake a 9″ x 13″ two-layer sheet cake and a 6″ x 2″ single layer. Fill, ice and assemble on cake board.

2. On 6″ layer, pipe tube 22 top crown border and tube 17 bottom star border. For base border of sheet cake, pipe a tube 18 plume design, an upright shell at corners and stars. Pipe tube 17 top shell border and stars down corners. Secure bachelor buttons on mounds of icing and trim with tube 66 leaves. Pipe message with tube 2. Add candles in clear holders. The 6″ layer serves three, the sheet cake serves 24.

Pinball pastime

If he plays pinball, this spectacular showpiece cake is for him! Patterns are in *Celebrate! V Pattern Book*.

1. Do back panel a few days in advance. Cut a 9″ x 13″ x 1″ piece of styrofoam and ice with royal icing. Trace pattern onto it. Outline design with tube 2 and royal icing combined with an equal amount of piping gel. Dry. Mix tinted piping gel with an equal amount of water and fill areas, using a cut cone.

2. Make Color Flow pieces, outlining with tube 2. Dry. For side buttons, cut a regular size marshmallow into thirds and flatten two pieces with fingers, then paint with thinned royal icing. For plunger, paint a 4″ dowel rod with thinned royal icing. Pipe end grip and ring of plunger with tube 6 and flatten. Pipe spring with tube 4. Dry.

3. Bake, fill and ice a 9″ x 13″ two-layer sheet cake. Place on cake board, then trace pattern onto top. Outline and fill areas the same as back panel. Secure Color Flow pieces to cake with dots of icing, elevating bumpers on miniature marshmallows. Attach back panel to cake with dowels as shown in diagram below. Cover sides of cake, sides and back of back panel with tube 16 stars. Place plunger in position and pipe red ball at end with tube 6. Secure buttons to side of cake. Insert Push-in holders into cake side and serve to 24.

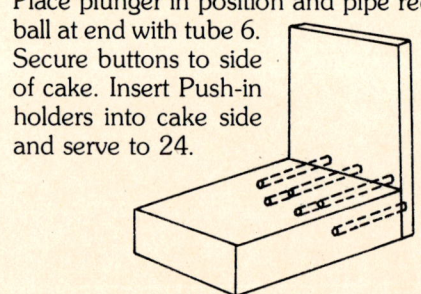

26

Men's masterpieces

Here are cakes that cater to the things he enjoys in his leisure time. These easy-to-serve sheet cakes are just as appropriate for a young man in his teens as for his father.

Not much time to decorate, but want to show your love for your special man in a very special way? Here are three stunning new cakes from the Sugar Plum Shop—each will be a delight to him— each will make you proud to present it!

Chocolate monogram
Quick & clever

It's easy to make this personalized cake just for him using only one tube!

1. Bake a two-layer 10″ round cake. Fill and ice with chocolate icing and set on cake board or serving tray. Divide side of cake into eighths, then pipe tube 16 scrolled shapes at each division and trim with stars. Fill bottom border between scrolls with stars. On top border, pipe a curved shell above each scroll, then fill between them with stars.

2. The monogram is his alone and you create it yourself! The initial for the last name is in the center—make it 4″ high. The other two initials go on either side of it—make them 3″ high. Practice first on the back of a 10″ pan, then lightly mark letters on top of cake. Pipe with tube 16, then add curved flourishes and stars to letters with same tube. Insert Push-In holders into cake, add the candles and serve to 14.

Birthday calendar
Quick & clever

Honor his day in a big way with this easy-to-serve sheet cake. A candle marks the special day, large round tubes make it a breeze to decorate.

1. Bake a two-layer 11″ x 15″ sheet cake. Fill, ice and set on cake board. Pipe tube 20 bottom shell border, tube 16 top shell border. Add message to side of cake with tube 9.

2. Divide cake top, within top border, for calendar, using his month as a guide. Divide long sides into seven, short sides into five or six, depending on the month. Mark lines in icing for squares with a piece of light cardboard. Use *Celebrate! V* patterns for numbers or pipe them freehand. Pipe lines with tube 5 and numbers with tube 7—leave his birthday blank. Add tube 3 name of month in one of left-over squares, pipe tube 5 hearts in others. In birthday square, insert a slim taper into cake. Add a few tube 193 drop flowers and candy hearts mounted on florists' wire. Serves 35.

Loving birthday wishes
Quick & clever

Give a great big birthday wish with this joyful cake trimmed with hearts. It is piped quickly with large tubes.

1. Pipe name in block letters on wax paper with royal icing and tube 22. Make them about 2″ high. When dry, remove from wax paper, turn over and attach toothpicks extending from the bottoms of the letters with icing. Pipe letters again on back and dry.

2. Bake 6″ and 10″ two-layer square tiers. Fill, ice and assemble on cake board. Cover sides of tiers with tube 1D vertical stripes, alternating red and orange, then add tube 504 hearts. Pipe red halves of hearts on orange stripes—orange halves on red stripes. On lower tier, pipe tube 12 bottom ball border and tube 9 top ball border. On upper tier pipe tube 12 bottom ball border and tube 8 top ball border. Insert slim tapers into top of cake and push toothpicks on the piped letters into cake. Serves 28.

Sugar Plum signature cake
(shown on page 5)

This lovely cake was specially decorated by Norman Wilton to set the theme of the Sugar Plum Shop. Using graceful techniques from the past, it sends a traditional birthday greeting to someone very special.

1. Make flowers in advance—Easter lilies, violets, dogwood, roses and daffodils—or any combination you wish. This is the perfect cake for using extra flowers left from other cakes.

2. Bake a two-layer 12″ round cake with a firm pound cake batter (or any firm type of cake). Fill the layers, then secure to a cake board the same size as the cake. To cover with rolled fondant, first make a recipe of marzipan (page 159) and roll into a 22″ circle about ⅜″ thick. Brush cake with hot apricot glaze (heat apricot jam to boiling and strain). Place marzipan over cake, smooth with hands and trim excess at base. Make a recipe of rolled fondant (page 159). Roll out into a 24″ circle, ¼″ thick. Brush marzipan coating with apricot glaze and place fondant over cake. Smooth, then trim excess. Smooth again and trim bottom edge so it is perfectly even. Transfer cake carefully to a foil-covered cake board.

3. Use boiled icing for piped trims. For bottom border, pipe tube 172 stars and trim each with a tube 14 curve. Divide side of cake into twelfths along top edge and drop a string guideline from point to point. Following guideline, pipe tube 16 zigzag garlands, then add tube 4 strings and tube 16 rosettes. Pipe tube 4 zigzags and fleurs-de-lis on top of cake between the side garlands.

4. Pipe tube 4 curved stems, then pipe a crescent-shaped mound of icing on top of cake. Secure flowers with icing to mound and down side of cake. Trim with tube 67 leaves. Write the message with tube 2 and serve to 22.

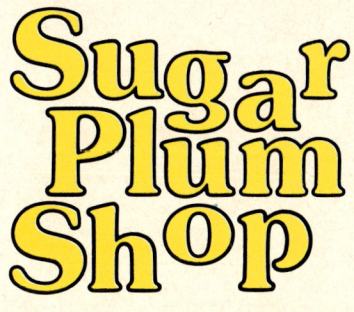

A birthday aquarium

Are tropical fish his passion? He'll love this ingenious cake, surprisingly quick to decorate.

1. Make marzipan fish (recipe on page 159) using *Celebrate! V* patterns. Place fish for side of cake on curved surface. Trim with pieces of marzipan, attaching with egg white or piping gel. Pipe additional trims of fish with tube 2. White part of eye is piped with tube 10 and then a thin circle of marzipan cut with tube 7 is placed on top. Dry.

For large fish on top, cut one and trim with pieces of marzipan. Cut a second fish and push toothpicks into lower fins. Brush with egg white or gel and lay first fish on top of it. Place on flat surface, pipe message and trims with tube 2 and dry. Cut snail, pipe tube 1 trims and dry on flat surface.

2. Bake a 10″ x 2″ single-layer cake for base, an 8″ x 6″ square, three-layer cake for aquarium. Ice 10″ cake, insert dowel rods, clipped level with top for support and place on 12″ square cake board. Fill 8″ layers, place on cardboard square the same size, and ice with boiled icing. Set on 10″ cake.

3. Pipe bulb borders on all edges of 10″ cake with tube 7. Insert four tall, thin tapers into base cake right up against corners of aquarium cake. Match icing to candles and pipe tube 11 borders on top and base of aquarium cake.

4. Push toothpicks on large fish into top of cake. Pull up "splashes" of boiled icing around lower fins. Push remaining fish into icing on sides of cake, then pipe tube 2 bubbles. Pipe tube 1 plants in lower corners of cake and attach snail with a dot of icing. Add tube 2 name on side of base cake. Base cake serves ten, aquarium cake serves about 16.

Front runner

Rain or shine, does he run every morning? This is the cake for him. Patterns are in *Celebrate! V Pattern Book* (there's even a pattern for a girl runner included for female participants).

1. Make a recipe of gum paste (page 13) and roll out. Lay patterns on gum paste and cut around them with a sharp knife. Dry on a flat surface. Transfer pattern details to gum paste. Using Color Flow icing straight from the batch, outline the figures with tube 1. Dry, then flow in the areas using a cut cone. Dry. Secure toothpicks extending from feet on backs of figures with royal icing. Cut a 2½″ x 8″ oval plaque from gum paste and dry. Pipe tube 2 message on it.

2. Pipe drop flowers with tubes 224 and 225. Add tube 2 centers and dry.

3. Bake a 6″ x 4″ round and a 6″ x 4″ square, two-layer cakes. Fill each, then cut round cake in half. Assemble on an oval cake board, 14″ x 8″, with a round half-cake on either side of square cake to create oval. Ice the assembled cake.

Divide side of cake into sixteenths. At each division, pipe a pair of tube 45 vertical stripes. Pipe tube 6 bottom ball border and tube 4 top ball border. Place plaque on cake top and edge with tube 2 beading. Insert toothpicks on runners' feet into cake top. Trim cake with drop flowers and add tube 65 leaves. Insert Push-In holders and trim with flowers and leaves. Serves 14.

Cheer your man with a birthday cake that expresses his favorite hobby

Please a man

Decorate a cake using his favorite flavor—chocolate. No frills, just simple, masculine cakes with a lot of appeal.

Chocolate sweetheart
Quick & clever

Send loving birthday greetings with this cake topped by chocolate hearts.

1. Mold hearts. First temper the chocolate. Heat water in the bottom of a 1½ quart double boiler to 175°F. Remove from heat, place cut-up chocolate, one cup at a time, in top half of boiler. Stir occasionally until melted and at a temperature of 110°F. Remove top pan and cool chocolate until stiff. To mold, reheat dark chocolate to 90°—92°F. Reheat milk chocolate to 86°—88°F before using.

Do not attempt to work with chocolate in hot, humid weather. Summer coating, which has a higher melting point, should be substituted. Summer coating does not need to be tempered.

Use heart cupcake pan as a mold. Be sure it is clean and dry by polishing the inside surface with a soft cloth. Have mold at room temperature. Pour in tempered chocolate to fill hearts (fill all six indentations in pan). Place in refrigerator just until chocolate is no longer liquid. Remove from refrigerator and hollow out with a teaspoon. Put back in refrigerator until chocolate is completely cooled and hardened. Turn pan over on a piece of cardboard and tap each indentation to remove the molded hearts.

2. Bake, fill and ice a 12" x 4" two-layer hexagon cake. On each side, use a 2½" heart cookie cutter as a pattern press. Pipe scrolls on heart shapes with tube 18. Pipe tube 18 shells around top and base of cake and down corners. Insert a candle in top of cake and trim base of it with tube 18 shells.

3. Position molded chocolate hearts on top of cake. Trim three with tube 2 script and the others with tube 129 drop flowers and tube 65 leaves. Add drop flowers and leaves to scroll designs on sides of cake. Serves 20.

Chocolate daisy
Quick & clever

This striking cake is very easy to create with quick-method daisies piped directly on the cake.

1. Bake, fill and ice a 9" x 13" x 4" two-layer sheet cake. Place on serving tray. Make daisy petals with tube 20, centers with tube 16. Pipe a half-daisy on each corner of cake at base. Divide the areas between them on the short sides of the cake into thirds and on the long sides into fifths. Pipe a half-daisy at each marked division.

2. On top of cake, pipe daisies in a semi-circle. Insert a birthday candle into each one. Pipe message with tube 16, then add tube 18 top shell border. Serve to 24 guests.

Chocolate mint
Quick & clever

Covered with mint green icing and trimmed with chocolate-covered mint patties, this cake is quick to do and looks stunning. He'll love it—and you.

1. Bake a cake in the Ring-Shaped Mold. Ice, then place on serving tray. Cover top of cake with tube 18 stars. Secure mint patties to side of cake with icing, then pipe tube 18 stars to fill the spaces between the patties.

2. Pipe tube 2 lettering on the patties at the front of the cake—one letter on each. Secure a fat candle to the serving tray with icing in the center hole of the cake. If candle is too short, place crumpled aluminum foil under it before setting in the hole. Serves twelve guests.

Sugar Plum Shop

Sugar Plum Shop

Marigold

Bring sunshine to her day by wreathing her cake with these golden ruffled flowers. A quickly piped but very effective border sets off the blooms.

1. First pipe the flowers in royal icing. You'll need about three dozen. Use nail number 7 and tube 103. Pipe a ruffled circle near edge of nail, lifting tube for upstanding effect. Pipe two more circles within it, making each more upstanding than the last. Fill center with petals that stand almost straight up. Dry the flowers.

2. Bake a 12″ two-layer round cake. Chill, fill and ice, then set on a 16″ serving tray or cake board. Pipe a tube 19 bottom shell border. Divide top edge of cake into twelfths. Drop tube 14 strings from each point, then center each string with a tube 19 upright shell. Add tube 16 rosettes, and pipe rosettes on top edge of cake where the strings meet. Complete the top border with tube 16 shells.

3. Lightly mark a curve on top of cake and print message with tube 3. Complete the curve with candles. Arrange marigolds on cake top, tilting each on a mound of icing. Circle the base of the cake with a wreath of flowers, then trim all with tube 67 leaves. This sunny creation serves 22.

Sixteen sweet daisies . . .

circle each tier of this fresh-as-a-daisy cake. Make it for a girl who's just turned 16, or for any lady you love.

1. Pipe 16 large daisies in royal icing with tube 125. Pipe tube 3 centers and flatten with a fingertip dipped in tinted granulated sugar. Dry within a curved surface. Pipe 16 smaller daisies with tube 104. Do centers same as for large daisies and dry within curved surface. Pipe a tube 5 royal icing spike on center back of all daisies.

2. Bake the tiers. Base tier consists of two 10″ round layers, each about 1½″ high, plus a layer baked in a 10″ top bevel pan. Top tier is an 8″ round layer and a layer baked in an 8″ top bevel pan. Fill the layers and set each tier on a cake circle the same size.

Ice the top and slanted edge of each tier green, and pat with damp sponge. Ice the sides smoothly in white. Set lower tier on tray and insert ¼″ dowel rods, clipped off level with top. Assemble the tiers.

3. Pipe a tube 32 bottom shell border on base tier. Use tube 16 for all other borders. Divide top edges of both tiers into sixteenths. Drop tube 8 stems from marks on sides of lower tier, tube 7 stems on upper tier. Push in spiked daisies on mounds of icing at top of stems. Add tube 66 leaves and a crown of candles set in clear holders. Serves 24, or cut each tier into 16 slices so that everyone receives a daisy.

Morning Glory

Heavenly blue flowers tell her what a glorious girl she is!

1. Make 20 royal icing morning glories in advance. Line a 1⅝″ two-piece lily nail with foil. Pipe a tube 104 coil of white icing in well of nail. Pipe a tube 103 ruffle around coil with blue icing and smooth two colors together with a damp artist's brush. Use tube 1 to pipe five lines from center of flower to edge, then pipe a tube 2 pistil. Lift foil from nail and dry. Pipe a tube 10 royal icing spike on backs of six flowers.

2. Bake a two-layer 10″ square cake. Fill layers, ice top green and sides white. Set on cake board. Divide each side of cake into eighths at top edge. Connect marks on opposite sides by pressing surface with a light cardboard. Use these lines as guides to pipe tube 47 lattice. Do bottom shell border with tube 19, top border with tube 16.

3. Insert tall tapers into cake. Arrange morning glories on top of cake, tilting each on a mound of icing. Push spiked flowers into side of cake. Add tube 67 leaves and a few tube 1 tendrils. Your glorious cake is finished and ready to serve 20 at the party!

Delight a lady

by heaping her birthday cake with her favorite flowers. This page starts a parade of pretty cakes trimmed just for her with all the feminine curves and flourishes she loves. (See Commonsense, starting on page 149, for a flower refresher course.)

Fresh flowered cakes from the Sugar Plum Shop to mark a lady's birthday

Flowers can take many forms to brighten a cake—here are just five. Read about them, starting clockwise at upper left of facing page.

Time to Celebrate!
Quick & clever

Sweeten a clock cake with wild roses. (Good idea for a New Year's cake, too.)

1. Pipe wild roses with tube 103 and royal icing. Add tube 2 stamens and dry in curved form. Bake two single-layer tiers, 10" round and 10" square. Set each on cardboard cake base, ice and mark sides with decorating comb. Insert a circle of ¼" dowels in square tier, and clip off level with top. Ice two stacks of sugar cubes and set near back. Place round tier on square tier.

2. Do lettering with tube 2. Use Numeral cutters to mark numbers on clock. Pipe with tube 16 and add shells between them. Do clock hands and all borders with same tube. Trim with flowers on mounds of icing and conceal sugar cubes with a few flowers. Light the clock with tall tapers. Top tier serves seven, lower tier, ten guests.

A circle of chrysanthemums
Quick & clever

A pattern press makes it easy to pipe the stylized flowers.

1. Bake, fill and ice a two-layer 12" round cake. Set on serving tray and mark six designs, evenly spaced, on top of cake. Tint buttercream and fill in designs with tube 20 shells.

2. Write message with tube 2. Divide lower side into sixteenths and pull up tube 20 upright shells. Complete base border with tube 17 shells. Use the same tube to drop strings and twirl rosettes. Finish with a tube 17 top shell border. Insert a tall taper and present to 22 party guests.

A basket of blossoms

Pipe a pretty basket and fill it with sugar flowers to make Mom happy!

1. Mold the tinted sugar flowers in the Flower molds (recipe page 11). Add edible glitter to the mixture for sparkle. Bake, fill and ice an 8" two-layer cake. Place on serving tray. On top of cake, mark a basket shape, 3¼" wide at top, 2½" high. Mark a curve for handle.

2. Fill in basket shape with tube 9 and several layers of zigzag, first horizontal, then vertical. Smooth surface with a small spatula. Now weave the basket with tube 5. Add rope borders with same tube and pipe handle with tube 7. Add a ribbon bow with tube 103.

3. Pipe message with tube 2, base bulb border with tube 8, top and corner borders with tube 7. Now fill the basket with flowers, tilting each on a mound of icing. Trim with tube 67 leaves. Insert candles in Push-In holders. Serve this sweet surprise to twelve party guests.

Has she a green thumb?

Sprinkle her cake with flowers!

1. Bake cookies cut with Daisy cutters and one with the Giant Open Hand cutter. Outline with royal icing and tube 1, then thin the icing and flow in color areas with a cut cone. Pipe tube 4 centers on daisies and a tube 17 zigzag cuff on hand.

2. Bake, fill and ice a two-layer 9" x 13" sheet cake. (Bake a larger one if you expect a crowd.) Pipe a tube 3 message. Pipe bottom border with tube 20 half-daisy shells centered with rosettes. Pipe tube 18 top shell border. Arrange cookies on top of cake and secure a few on sides with icing. Serve this flowery treat to 24 guests.

One perfect rose . . .

all you need to trim the loveliest birthday cake a lady could receive!

1. Pipe the rose with tube 126 on a number 14 flower nail. Page 153 gives directions for the rose, piped the Wilton Way. If you are using buttercream icing, freeze the rose until serving time.

2. Bake, fill and ice a two-layer oval cake. Set on an oval cake board cut 12" x 10". Divide side of cake into tenths and mark about 1" up from base. Pipe tube 1 script on cake side.

3. Pipe a double tube 6 bulb border around bottom of cake. Swing tube 104 ruffled garlands from marked points, then pipe tube 14 zigzag garland. Add tube 2 strings, hearts and dots.

Frame top with a tube 5 bulb border, then pipe one on either side of it. Pipe tube 2 scallops within border. Pipe a tube 7 main stem and smaller stems with tube 5. Add tube 1 thorns and tube 67 leaves. Place rose on a mound of icing. A radiant little masterpiece that serves twelve.

He'll enjoy this *Quick & clever* cake as much as his favorite sport!

Surprise him with a racquet ball cake (or bake one for a lady enthusiast). It's quick to do—the clever trim is piped right on the cake!

1. Bake a single-layer 9" x 13" sheet cake. Ice smoothly and set on cake board, then transfer *Celebrate! V* pattern to top. Outline raquet and ball with tube 3 and royal icing, then pipe tube 2 lattice strings. Add string at base of handle. Now fill in ball and racquet frame with thinned icing and pipe message with tube 3.

2. Divide short sides of cake into fifths at top edge, longer sides into sixths. Mark points near base of cake midway between marks at top. Pipe tube 16 lines from mark to mark in "V" shapes. Add zigzag borders at base and top of cake with same tube. Now finish base border with tube 10 balls. Frame with candles in Push-In holders. It's a winner! Serves twelve players.

BIG BEAUTIFUL DOLLS, *continued*

cakes on each side. Push tall tapers into center of cake and surround with drop flowers. Now push marshmallows into tops of half-Wonder Molds.

3. Pipe tube 9 arms from shoulders of dolls, meeting on sides of cake. Mark apron area on each doll. Cover dresses with tube 14 stars up to aprons. Pipe tube 101 ruffles at bottom of aprons and fill in with white stars. Over-pipe sleeves. Cover bonnets with stars and add a tube 101 ruffle to each, and to necklines. Do hair, features, bows and buttons with tube 2. Pipe tube 2 stems on side of cake, starting where arms meet. Top with drop flowers and add tube 101 bows.

Each little doll serves a delighted guest—the square cake serves twelve.

Big dolls bring gifts

This cheerful trio will bring smiles to everyone's face! You'll be surprised at the way they're shaped—

1. Bake three cakes in the bowling pin pans! Use a firm pound cake recipe. Chill, then fill with buttercream and fasten the two halves with toothpicks. Cut 2" off base of each cake. Cut cardboard cake bases to size, attach with icing to base of each cake and stand upright. Cover cakes with a thin coat of flesh-colored icing. Lightly mark face areas, about 2" down from top and waistline about 4" down. Pipe a few tube 33 royal icing drop flowers. Each gift is made of two sugar cubes, iced together. Pipe ribbons with tube 2.

2. Start with the yellow doll. Pipe feet with tube 12 and add tube 2 ties. Starting at bottom, cover skirt with tube 127 ruffles. Then fill area up to face with tube 15 stars. Attach present to front of doll with icing, then pipe tube 2A arms. Cover top of arms with stars, over-piping for puffy sleeves. Finish neckline with tube 4 beading. Pipe hair with tube 13 and press in flowers. Add tube 65 leaves. Pipe eyes with tube 5 and flatten with a fingertip. Smile is piped with tube 3. Attach a ribbon bow.

3. Follow the same steps to decorate the pink and green dolls—use your imagination to give each a different costume. Each doll serves ten.

Celebrate!
A BRIGHT NEW YEAR IN JANUARY AND FEBRUARY

Love in bloom.
Decorating directions, page 54

Fruit cakes

Outside it's chilly January, but inside it seems like summer when you serve these luscious, fruit-trimmed cakes. It's a marvelous way to make any day a special one!

Boxes of berries
Quick & clever

Why wait until the weather gets warm to serve juicy berries to your family? Do it right now with this cheerful cake.

1. Make marzipan (recipe on page 159). Tint a portion beige and roll out thin. Cut eight pieces for box sides, each 3" high, 4" wide at top, 3¾" wide at bottom. Cut eight 1" wide, 4" long strips for top edges of boxes. Cut eight more strips, ½" wide, 3⅞" long for remaining top edges on top of cake.

2. Bake and fill an 8" x 3" square, two-layer cake. Ice light chocolate, then press two marzipan box sides into wet icing on each side of cake. Brush piping gel on 1" top edges of box and press to cake sides so about ½" extends above the cake top. Press ½" box edges in icing on top of cake as pictured.

3. Pipe blueberries and gooseberries with tube 8 and figure piping technique. Keep tip of tube buried in icing while squeezing. Stop pressure, then pull away for rounded shapes. Pipe berries one on the other for a natural look. Add tube 1 dots to gooseberries and trim berries with tube 66 leaves. This little cake serves twelve.

Wreath it with raspberries
Quick & clever

So simple to decorate, so pretty to see!
1. Make tube 225 drop flowers with royal icing. Add tube 2 centers and dry.
2. Bake, fill and ice an 8" x 4" round, two-layer cake and place on a serving tray. Edge base with tube 20 shells.
3. Divide top edge of cake into eighths and secure three raspberry candies at each division and add clusters at base of cake with dots of icing. Add tube 66 leaves and drop flowers. Serve to ten.

Plant a cherry tree!
Quick & clever

Here's a happy, easy cake to brighten a winter day. Trim one to send to school on Washington's birthday!

1. Bake a 9" x 13" x 4" two-layer sheet cake and a 5" x 1½" round layer in Mini-Tier pan. Fill the sheet cake, ice and secure to cake board. Ice 5" layer and place on sheet cake for top of tree.
2. Pipe tree trunk with tube 18, then pipe top of tree with tube 66 leaves. Push cherry candies into wet icing and pipe more leaves around them. Pipe grass at base of tree with tube 66.
3. Pipe tube 16 shell borders around top and base of cake. Secure cherry candies at each corner on side of cake with dots of icing. Add tube 2 stems and tube 66 leaves. Serve to 24.

Strawberries and cream
Quick & clever

Marzipan strawberries, whipped cream and a pound cake make a special treat!
1. Pipe tube 225 royal icing drop flowers with tube 2 centers. Dry.
2. Make marzipan (recipe on page 159) and tint a portion red and one green. Form red marzipan into a ½" diameter cylinder and cut into 1" lengths. Roll each piece into a ball and pinch end to give it a berry shape. Roll lightly on a damp sponge, then in red granulated sugar. You will need 50 strawberries. Dip one end of a green-tinted toothpick into water, then into top of berry. Leave twelve without toothpicks.

Roll green marzipan thin and cut leaves and calyxes using Flower Garden large rose leaf cutters. Score veins with back of knife and dry within a curved surface. Brush backs of calyxes with water and press to berries, pushing over the inserted toothpicks.

3. Prepare Heart Bowl by securing a half-ball of styrofoam in it with icing. Cover styrofoam with a circle of green marzipan. Insert toothpicks on berries into styrofoam. Attach leaves and drop flowers with dots of icing.

4. Bake a pound cake in Ring-Shaped Mold. Brush with warm apricot glaze (heat apricot jam to boiling and strain), then place on serving tray. Pipe tube 22 stars at base of cake with stabilized whipped cream. (Recipe on page 159.) Place bowl of strawberries in center hole of cake. Secure six pairs of strawberries around cake side with icing, then add leaves and drop flowers. Serve this treat with whipped cream to 20.

Bring spring to the party with these pretty flower sheet cakes. They're fast and easy to trim. Bright blossoms make everyone forget the chilly winter winds.

Plan a little get-together for neighbors and friends—or create these pretty desserts just for the family. Each is an easy-to-serve sheet cake, each cuts into 24 servings, each is a real spirit-lifter for winter-weary souls.

Rosebuds all in a row
Quick & clever

Dainty, easy-to-make rosebuds are piped right on the cake for very quick decorating. This cake is fun to trim!

1. Bake, fill and ice a 9" x 13" x 4" two-layer sheet cake. Place on cake board and divide long sides into fourths, short sides into thirds. Lightly mark a vertical line at each division on cake sides with the edge of a light cardboard. Now mark diagonal lines on the cake top from one division on a long side to another division on the adjacent short side as pictured.
2. Pipe swirled rosettes on the marked diagonal lines on the cake top and on the vertical lines on the cake sides with tube 20. Pipe rosettes around the base of the cake with the same tube. Add neat tube 67 leaves to the rosettes. See how easy it is to create a beautiful cake in just a short time!

A spray of tulips
Quick & clever

Think of warmer weather with these beautiful springtime blossoms. They add a special touch and are so lovely to look at, so easy to pipe.

1. Bake, fill and ice a 9" x 13" x 4" two-layer sheet cake. Place on a foil-covered cake board. Pipe tube 20 bottom shell border.
2. On the top of the cake, pipe long tube 6 stems in a natural-looking spray arrangement. Pipe tulip flowers directly on the cake at the tops of the stems using tube 12. Beginning at the base of the flower, pipe the two outer petals first, then the center petal. Use heavy pressure to begin, then reduce pressure gradually as you move toward the top of the petal. Add long ruffled leaves with tube 113, starting at the base of the stems. Pipe a tube 17 top shell border and the lovely cake is complete!

Sweet peas twine on lattice
Quick & clever

Dainty lattice and cascades of sweet peas sweeten this spring creation. It's a happy cake to forecast a delightful spring to come!

1. Make many sweet peas in advance using tube 104 and royal icing. Hold tube at 45° angle with wide end on surface. For center petal, squeeze, lift slightly, relax pressure, come back to surface and stop pressure. Set tube to left and right and repeat motions for side petals. Pipe smaller sweet peas with tube 103. Dry.
2. Bake, fill and ice a 9" x 13" x 4" two-layer sheet cake. Place on board. Mark *Celebrate!* V pattern (or draw your own) in the icing on the top of the cake. Pipe lattice from the pattern line to the edges of the cake with tube 2. Corner areas will not match, but flowers will cover them. Add tube 5 beading around the inside and outside edges of the lattice.
3. Secure single sweet peas in four neat rows in the center of the piped lattice design on the cake top with dots of icing. Add a tube 65 leaf to each. With a large round tube, pipe a mound of icing at each corner on the top of the cake. Secure sweet peas to the mounds with dots of icing, adding a few flowers extending down onto the sides of the cake at the corners. Trim with tube 65 leaves.
4. Pipe tube 7 ball border around the base of the cake. Divide the long sides of the cake into fifths, the short sides into fourths and mark. Pipe a tube 104 swag from point to point. Add a flower at the top points of the swag on a dot of icing and trim with a tube 65 leaf. Your pretty cake is completed —and it was so easy to do!

Flower cakes

50

A valentine decorated decades ago... now done again and just as sweet

"Here is a uniquely beautiful valentine cake that can be made very quickly..."

When Norman Wilton wrote these words years ago he pointed out one of the identifying marks of the Wilton-American method of decorating—make the cake beautiful, but do it in an efficient time-saving way.

Perhaps you remember this cake, shown in a Wilton book published in 1953. We recreated it, just as Mr. Wilton originally decorated it, to show you how techniques developed in the past are just as effective today.

1. Start by baking a 10″ round two-layer cake. Set one layer on a 10″ cake circle, spread filling and top with second layer. Now, using plenty of buttercream, ice the cake smoothly. (One of the secrets of a smooth finish is to cover the cake with a thin coating of icing first to seal in any crumbs.)

2. Do the cake-top heart first. Fold a piece of parchment paper in half and cut out a pattern, 5½″ high, 5½″ wide. Lay the pattern on the cake and trace around it with a toothpick. Now outline the heart with a heavy line piped with tube 5. Let this set up while you transfer the cake to a serving tray and warm about a half-cup of poured fondant. (Page 159.) Tint the fondant a deep rose and pour it into the outlined heart.

3. Surround the cake base with puffy upright shells, using tube 32. Join every other shell with tube 4 double strings, then go back and connect remaining shells with strings. (To pipe graceful strings, keep the work at eye level and work in an even rhythm.) Add twirls of icing at points of string.

Spatula stripe a decorating cone, fitted with tube 124, with deep pink and fill with pastel pink icing. Pipe a ruffle around the heart and a curving border around the top edge of the cake. Do the border by piping a curve, jiggling hand slightly, then going into a curve again. The color striping accents the ruffles and curves. Pipe the name with tube 2. Flourishes are made by pausing slightly and moving hand back and forth as you pipe letters.

4. Now add the flower sprays. These gracefully curved arrangements are almost a hallmark of the Wilton way. First pipe curved stems. Spatula stripe a cone fitted with tube 104 with deep color, fill with pink icing for the rosebuds. Pipe them right on the cake. Hold wide end of tube on surface, narrow end straight up, and press out a cupped petal. Touch tube just inside right edge of petal and squeeze lightly as you lift tube slightly. Hesitate for an instant, continuing pressure, and icing will roll into a spiraled inner petal. Move back to right and down. Bring hand straight over for flat outer petal. Finish flower by pulling out points with tube 3 for calyx.

Thin the icing to pipe perky tube 67 leaves, lifting tube so points tilt up.

Your sweet valentine is complete—and it is proof of another point that is emphasized in the Wilton method: all decorating, however simple, must be executed perfectly. Only repeated practice will give you the skill that can turn out a beautifully decorated cake, quickly.

Valentine bouquets
Quick & clever

The little square cake at left teaches the same lessons as the cake on the opposite page. Use time saving methods wherever possible, and execute all details perfectly.

1. Pipe royal icing drop flowers with tube 193. Pipe tube 2 centers and dry. (Many decorators pipe extra royal icing flowers for a cake and store them—then they are ready for any quick project.) Bake, fill and ice an 8″ square two-layer cake. Bake a cake in the Heart Minicake pan, ice and place on top of square.

2. Pipe tube 16 shell borders, then lightly mark a curve on top of cake and pipe tube 2 message. Use the same tube to pipe curving stems on heart cake and at corners on cake sides. Attach flowers on mounds of icing, then pipe bows with tube 102. Finish with tube 65 leaves. A pretty treat that serves twelve.

Golden Oldies

You don't need to have passed the half-century mark to know the words of these songs—they're being sung on college campuses everywhere! These cakes speak love in a light-hearted, very unsentimental way.

It had to be you
Tell him you love him still with a flowery heart! Just make royal icing drop flowers with tubes 35, 225 and 131 (or use flowers you've stored). Fill and ice a two-layer 8″ square cake and lightly mark a 5″ heart, 6″ wide on the top. Pipe message with tube 3, then fill the heart with flowers secured with icing. Add a few tube 65 leaves. Cover the sides with rosy stripes piped with tube 1D and press in more flowers for base border. Finish the top edge with tube 14 and present it to your valentine. Serves twelve.

You're the tops!
Top a little tower of a cake with Mickey Mouse!* Mold him in sugar and paint in bright colors using the method on page 11. Ice and assemble a cake baked in the Heart Mini-tier pans. Edge the tiers with tube 16 shells and drape with tube 14 string. Add red candy hearts. Cut a 1½″ heart from red paper and print message with tube 1. Attach to Mickey's hand with icing. As exciting as the Eiffel Tower! Serves twelve.

My heart belongs to Daddy
Tell him so with this double heart cake! Bake, fill and ice a two-layer 9″ heart cake, ice a heart cupcake and set on top. Pipe hearts for base border with tube 10 and pipe tube 16 stars between them. Do the top shell border with tube 16 and pipe a bold gold arrow with the same tube. Outline the little heart with tube 1. Put on the records and serve to twelve lovers.

I won't dance...
flowers and a top hat remind us of that famous couple on the late show. Trim this fast, funny cake for your favorite partner. Pipe tubes 225 and 35 royal icing drop flowers, dry and mount on wire stems (see Commonsense, starting on page 149). Twist stems together and add a ribbon bow. Bake, fill and ice a two-layer 10″ round cake. Pipe tube 3 message. Use tube 17 for all decorating. Mark side of cake with a 2″ heart cutter and pipe fluffy hearts. Do reverse shell base border and shell top border. Set Top Hat and Cane, accompanied by bouquet, on cake. This tuneful treat serves 14.

*Walt Disney's Mickey Mouse. © Walt Disney Productions.

Trim a cake with ruffles and ribbon, roses and bows, to show your valentine how much you care

Fill a basket with roses

An enchanting way to greet your love on February 14.

1. Make handle first in royal icing. Tape *Celebrate! V* pattern to stiff board and tape wax paper over it. Pipe a tube 6 line on pattern and over-pipe twice. When dry, pipe two tube 6 lines in indentations of triple lines, then a final line. Dry, then attach 4" pieces of florists' wire to underside of handle with icing to reinforce. Pipe a double and a single line of icing on underside of handle. Dry thoroughly.

2. Pipe royal icing roses and buds with tubes 104 and 103. Pipe forget-me-nots with tube 101 and add tube 1 centers. Trace a 3¼" heart cutter on red paper, glue a 6" length of florists' wire on center back extending from point of heart and glue a second paper heart over the wire. Write a tube 1 message on heart, then edge with a tube 101 ruffle and tube 3 beading.

3. Bake and fill a two-layer oval cake. Chill, then taper sides with a sharp knife to a slightly smaller base. Ice cake, then pipe tube 4 basket weaving. Vertical lines are double, horizontal lines triple for wicker look. Add a tube 17 rope border at base, tube 21 border at top. Carefully set handle on basket on mounds of icing. Mound icing on top of cake and arrange flowers. Trim with tube 66 leaves and insert heart. Tuck

an Angelino in the basket. Wire a fluffy bow to the handle and twine the ends around the curve. With royal icing attach two plastic doves. This dainty confection serves twelve.

Tie up a heart, *Quick & clever*

One of the sweetest cakes you could trim, especially suitable for a man.
1. Bake a two-layer cake in 9" Happiness Heart pans. Fill and set on cake base cut to match. Ice with white buttercream, let icing crust, then cover with pink poured fondant (recipe page 159).
2. Let fondant set, then pipe a double tube 2B ribbon diagonally across cake. Start from center of cake top and bring down to base on either side. Pipe two 3" lengths of ribbon on wax paper and freeze. When hard, notch the ends with a scissors and lay on cake top. Use tube 2 to pipe freehand embroidery and picot edges. Pipe a cluster of tube 22 rosette "rosebuds" on cake and add a few tube 66 leaves. Finish cake with a tube 8 bulb border. Serve to twelve.

Ruffle a sheet cake

1. Pipe drop flowers in royal icing with tube 225, add tube 2 centers and dry. Make the pretty ornament by gluing a Standing Cherub to a Petite Heart Base, then gluing a Seed Pearl Heart behind him. Attach a fluffy ribbon bow. Cut a 1" heart from red paper, letter name, and add beading with tube 1. When dry, attach to cherub's hand.
2. Bake, fill and ice a two-layer 9" x 13" sheet cake. Pipe tube 16 shells at base and top. Divide short sides of cake into fourths and mark about 1½" up from bottom. Divide longer sides into sixths. Drop string guidelines and pipe curving tube 125 ruffles. Add tube 3 beading.

Using base ruffles as guide, mark curves on top of cake about 1" from edge. Follow curves to pipe tube 125 ruffles, then pipe a second layer of ruffles within the first. Add tube 3 beading and write message with same tube. Set ornament on cake and trim with a few flowers on dots of icing. Cluster more flowers on corners of cake. A lovely centerpiece that serves 24.

Winter pleasures

Off to sunny isles

Send travelers off on their cruise or trip to Hawaii with this colorful cake trimmed with pineapples and hibiscus.

1. Make frilly hibiscus flowers in advance in royal icing. Line a 1¼" lily nail with foil. Starting deep in nail, pipe a tube 101 petal, narrow at base, then wider as you move out to edge. Jiggle hand to ruffle the petal, then move back to base. Repeat for five petals. Pull out a tube 2 stamen from center of flower and top with tube 1 yellow dots. Dry and pipe tube 5 royal icing spikes on the backs of most of the flowers.

2. Bake an 8" x 4" square, two-layer cake and two half-eggs in the Egg Mini-cake pan for pineapples. Fill and ice the square cake and place on a foil-covered cake board. Pipe tube 22 base shell border and trim each shell with a tube 102 ruffle. Pipe tube 16 reverse shell top border. Trim a little off of the wide ends of the half-egg cakes. Ice and place on top of square cake.

3. Fit a decorating bag with tube 83, then stripe the bag with a wide stripe of brown icing and fill with gold icing. Cover pineapples with tube 83 dots, piping them the same way as stars. Pipe long tube 326 leaves at the tops of the pineapples. Attach flowers to top and sides of cake in a cascade. Trim with tube 66 leaves. Pipe tube 3 message on the side of the cake. Serve to twelve.

Cross country!

Make this cake for an after-skiing party. Serve it in front of the fireplace with hot chocolate and friendly talk.

1. Make marzipan skiers in advance. (Recipe is on page 159.) Each figure is about 5" tall. Follow the diagram at left for creating the figures and assembling them. Use toothpicks for support and for ski poles. Model torso, then legs and attach. Add socks and shoes. Next model a ball for head and attach the hat. Make the part of the scarf around the neck and attach to torso, then add head. Assemble arms, cuffs and mittens, then secure to torso. Roll out marzipan and cut ¾" x 4" skis. Prop pointed tips and dry. Now add buttons, scarf ends, skis and ski poles. Pipe hair and features with tube 2. Brush skiers with glaze (see page 159) and sprinkle with edible glitter.

2. Make pine trees on parchment cones 7" to 9" high. Ice with royal icing, then pipe tube 16 upright shells at intervals on cones to give branch effect. Pull out foliage all over the trees with tube 74. Sprinkle trees heavily with edible glitter, then dry.

3. Bake a 9" x 13" x 4" two-layer sheet cake. Fill and place on cake board. Swirl on boiled icing. Edge cake with tube 7 balls, then sprinkle heavily with edible glitter. Place skiers on top of cake and arrange trees. Serve this winter treat to 24 happy skiers.

Greet the new year with a joyous at home party

Happy New Year!

A gay little New Year formally attired, dances on this happy cake.

1. Glue a Top Hat on a Dancing Angel and attach the Cane to his hand. Trim with ribbons and a drop flower.

2. Bake a single-layer 6" round tier and a two-layer 10" round tier. Fill and ice the 10" tier, ice the 6" tier and assemble on serving tray. On base tier, pipe a tube 8 bottom bulb border and trim with tube 4 balls. Edge top of tier with tube 7 bulbs. On upper tier, pipe a tube 6 bulb border with tube 4 balls and scallops. Pipe message on side of tier with tube 2. Secure figure to top of cake with icing. Divide lower tier side into sixths and mark.

3. Tint icing in vivid colors and pipe the balloons with tube 12. Use varying pressure to achieve different sizes. Pipe a cluster of balloons at each mark on lower tier and add tube 1 strings. Heap balloons around base of figure. Serve to 17 merry makers.

It's almost midnight!

A real extravaganza of a cake to welcome in a bright new year! Baroque gum paste designs frame the clock.

1. Make gum paste trims first (recipe page 13). Follow general directions in the instruction book that comes with the Baroque molds. Tint gum paste gold and mold four Scrolls and dry flat. When dry, pipe tube 1 royal icing lettering and spikes on the backs. Mold four Classic Shells. Trim off side curves and dry flat. Prop the curved edges of the trimmed shells with cotton for uptilted look and dry. Mold four Mantle designs and trim off center fleurs-de-lis. Dry the fleurs-de-lis around the corners of a square pan. Dry side curves flat, then mold four more Mantle designs, trim as before and attach back-to-back to dried side curves (booklet tells how).

From untinted gum paste, mold four Mantle designs, trim off center fleurs-de-lis and dry flat.

Use tube 103 and royal icing to pipe many sweet peas. Dry.

2. Bake a 12" x 3" two-layer square tier and an 8" x 4" two-layer tier. Fill, ice and assemble on cake board. Transfer *Celebrate! V* clock pattern to top of cake, and do lettering on side of base tier with tube 2. Pipe bottom shell border on base tier with tube 18. Cover top of tier with tube 1 cornelli. Pipe reverse shell top border with tube 16.

On top tier, pipe tube 17 bottom shells, tube 14 reverse shells on top.

3. Now add the festive decorations. Outline clock numbers and hands with tube 1 and royal icing, then flow in thinned icing. Outline circle of clock with tube 2 scallops and dots. 1" in from each edge of top tier, pipe tube 9 lines. Attach all gum paste designs with mounds of icing. Set tilted Classic Shells on corners of top tier and secure side curves against piped tube 9 lines. Push in Scrolls in the center of each side of tier. Set Mantle curves at angles on top of base tier, upper curves touching top tier. Attach fleurs-de-lis above them on corners of tier. Finally, secure untinted Mantle curves to corners of base tier. Arrange flowers on mounds of icing. This sunny cake serves 46.

A lesson in color, a lesson in lace, brought together on an exquisite cake

LOVE IN BLOOM *shown on page 39*
Start with a 9" x 13" sheet cake, add artful color, daintily piped lace, full blown roses and two sweet cherubs. Turn it into a centerpiece to celebrate a wedding, an anniversary, Valentine's day or any occasion where love is the reason. A little triumph of decorating!

Color sets the theme
Before starting any decorating project, keep in mind that color is the magic, essential ingredient that makes even the simplest cake beautiful. Here we are using bold scarlet in the heart shapes to set the analogous, closely related color scheme. A cool pink covers the little heart tier, the base tier is iced in warm rosy apricot, and all the lace is done in pastel apricot. Piped roses pick up all the hues and even the cupids' wings and sashes are pink. Their golden hair completes the color scheme.

Here is how we achieved the colors:
Red gum paste hearts—knead in Red-Red paste color.
Flesh colored gum paste for cupids—knead in liquid Copper plus a little Pink.
Cupids' wings and sashes—knead a little liquid Pink into gum paste.
Pink buttercream to cover heart tier—stir in a little liquid Pink.
Apricot buttercream for base tier—add Orange to pink icing above.
Apricot royal icing for lace pieces and cornelli—add just a touch of Pink liquid color to Orange-tinted egg white royal.
Royal icing roses—Use liquid colors —Pink for pink roses, Pink with a touch of Grape for deep rose, Orange plus Pink for apricot-colored flowers. For red roses use Red-Red *paste color.*
Gold royal icing for Cupids' hair—add Egg Yellow liquid color.

Make cupids first
Use the five-year-old molds from the People Mold set and mold the standing cupid as instruction booklet directs. To make the kneeling cupid, mold front half of legs, then back half. Brush surface of front half of legs with egg white, lift back half of legs from mold, and attach to front half (still in mold). Cut a "V" shape from back of knees, then carefully bend feet and lower legs up from mold, remove remaining leg and

torso from mold, and dry on wax paper in position. No wires are used. This figure is fragile, so use care in attaching upper torso.

Mold wings in Baroque Angelica mold as booklet directs. Mold wing areas only, omit face. Unmold, measure 1½" in from tips of wings, trim off and dry on wax paper, tilting wing tips up.

Cut heart shapes from gum paste using *Celebrate! V* patterns, and dry.

When cupid figures are dry, do hair and makeup. Attach arms as booklet directs and secure small hearts to hands with royal icing. Trim hearts with tube 1s and royal icing. Cut sashes from thinly rolled pink gum paste, using pattern. Carefully drape on cupids and dry, then attach wings. Brush a tiny piece of wet gum paste with egg white, press on back of cupid, brush again and attach wing. Prop with cotton balls and dry. Spray completed figures and larger hearts with two coats of clear acrylic.

Make lace pieces in advance
Here is the time-saving way to do this.

Trace *Celebrate! V* pattern in rows on transparent paper. Tape to stiff board and tape wax paper smoothly over. Now pipe with tube 1s and egg white royal icing. When dry, remove by sliding a small piece of paper under the lace pieces, starting at base. You will need about 125, but make extras.

Pipe the roses and buds
Use royal icing in varied tints and tubes 102, 103 and 104. Page 153 gives a refresher course in rose-making. When dry, pipe royal icing spikes on backs of half of the flowers (page 157).

Put the cake together
Bake a two-layer 9" x 13" sheet cake and a single-layer 6" heart. Set each on a matching cake base. Fill and ice the sheet cake, ice the heart cake and assemble. Drop string guidelines on side of cake for scallops as picture shows. Now pipe tube 1 cornelli, starting at marked scallops and covering top of sheet cake up to heart cake. Do this by piping meandering curved lines close together, none touching. Cornelli gives a delicate veil-like covering and softens the cake edges. Edge scallops with tube 2 beading and add fleurs-de-lis.

Edge base of sheet cake by first piping a tube 6 bulb border. Add upright shells above, then dots with tube 3. Edge the heart cake the same way, but use varied tints and tubes 4 and 2. Pipe a tube 2 bead border on top of heart.

Using patterns, cut clear plastic wrap in the three heart shapes for top of cake. Lay on cake, then cover with gum paste hearts. Edge large heart with tube 4 beading, two smaller hearts with tube 3. Do script with tube 1.

Now carefully add lace pieces to top of heart cake. Pipe a tiny line of royal icing on base of each piece, then set it just under bead border. Make sure lace pieces stand at uniform angle.

Ice marshmallows, attach to cake with icing at corners and attach roses to them. Add more flowers on mounds of icing. Attach remaining flowers and buds by pushing in spikes on mounds of icing. Add a few tube 66 leaves.

Attach lace to scallops the same as for heart cake. Set cupids on hearts, securing them the same as you attached wings. This masterpiece serves 27.

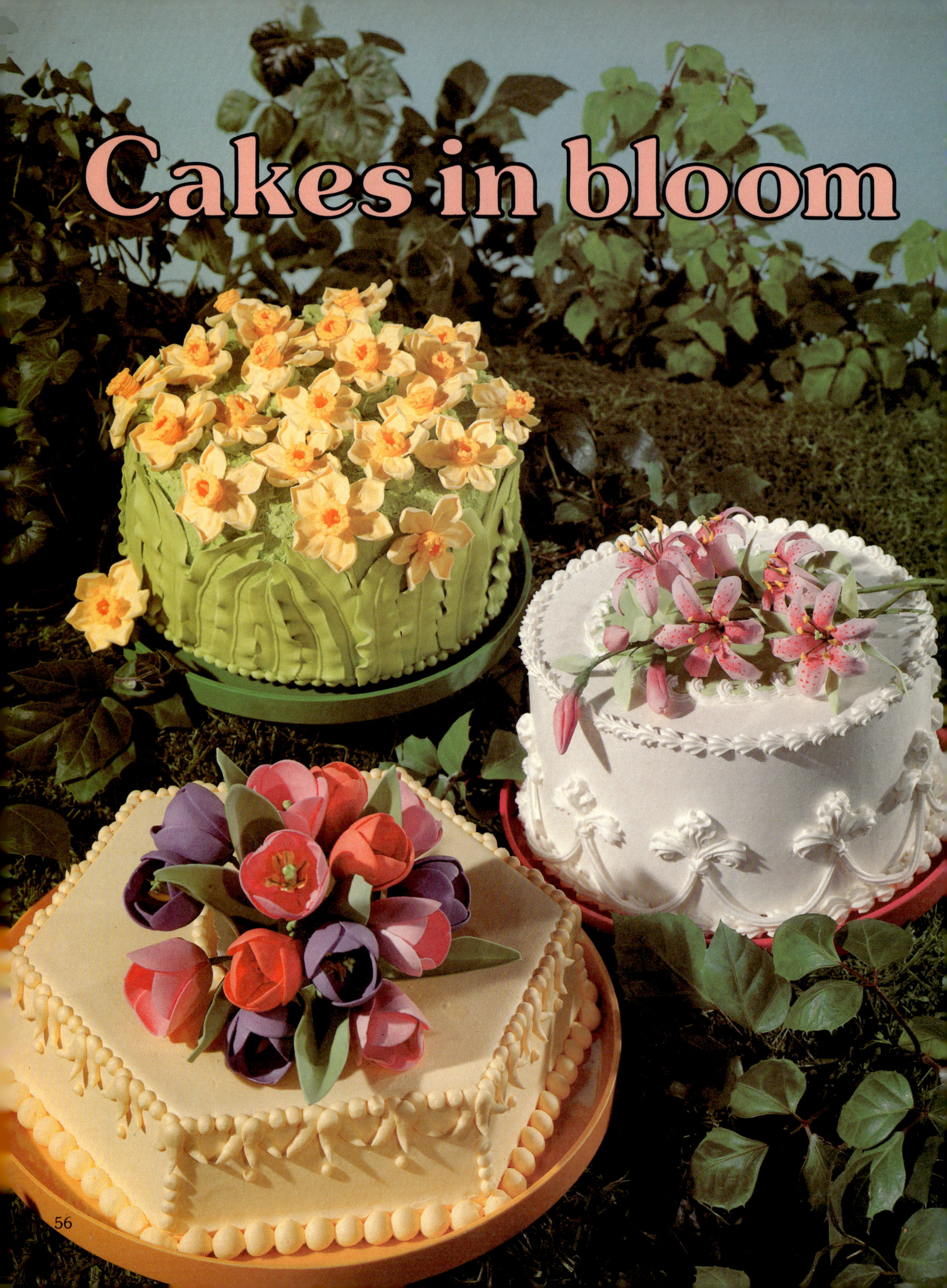

There's just no lovelier trim for a cake than flowers—and there are no lovelier flowers than those that bloom in the spring! Trim one of these small, but spectacular, cakes with spring blossoms. See how skillful piping can bring a bloom to life—and discover the amazing realism of gum paste flowers, quickly made, that become lasting little ornaments to keep or to give.

A golden garden

Here's a cake that's a little spring garden in itself. The sunny daffodils are easy to pipe.

1. Make about 25 royal icing daffodils in advance. Pipe six petals of equal size on nail number 13 with tube 124. Pinch each petal into a point while icing is wet with fingers dipped in cornstarch. Pipe center cup with tube 4 by pressing out a spiral coil of string. Edge cup with a tube 4 zigzag. Dry, then pipe a tube 7 spike on back of several flowers.

2. Bake, fill and ice an 8" x 4" round, two-layer cake. Pat with a clean, damp sponge. Place on a serving tray. Pipe tube 6 stems on side of cake, then pull up tube 114 leaves. Pipe bottom bulb border with tube 6. Attach daffodils to top of cake at perky angles on mounds of icing. Add a few flowers on side by pushing in spiked flowers on mounds of icing. The daffodil garden serves ten.

Lilies are the glorious trim

The Easter lily is one of the quickest flowers to make in gum paste—just one stamp of the cutter from the Flower Garden set shapes all the petals. Now see how you can create the rosy Red Champion lily with the same cutter. Mount the pretty pink spray on a separator plate and lift off before serving to present to an honored guest. She'll treasure it!

1. Make lilies and leaves in advance using the instruction booklet that accompanies the cutters for general directions. After shaping the lily into a cone, set it on a modeling stick, petals down, and cut between the petals about ½" to lengthen them. Bend the petals outward and place on a 1" thick piece of soft foam, face down. Clip hole at point. Curl the petals as booklet directs, then prop with cotton balls to create deeply curled reflexed petals and dry. Add the stems, then dust with powdered pastels and paint spots with pink liquid food color. Make leaves and buds. Tape into a spray.

2. Cover a 5½" separator plate from the Round Mini-tier set with green gum paste. Brush plate with egg white first. Attach spray with royal icing. Dry, then spray twice with clear acrylic.

3. Bake, fill and ice an 8" x 4" round two-layer cake. Set on serving tray. Center the separator plate on top of cake and push down until it is almost flat against the cake surface. Edge with tube 16 swirls. Pipe tube 18 base shell border. Divide side of cake into tenths. Drop tube 16 strings from point to point, then top intersections with tube 17 fleurs-de-lis and tube 16 stars. Add tube 16 top shell border. Lift off separator plate before serving to ten.

A bowl of brilliant tulips

Arrange gum paste tulips in a bowl to set within a ring cake. Lots of fun, not much time, a cake that says "spring!"

1. Make tulips and leaves using Flower Garden Cutter Set and instruction booklet. Tulips are very quick and showy flowers to make.

Glue a Filigree Bell to the top plate of a Petite Heart Base. Line bell with clear plastic, then fill with royal icing. Insert the tulips and leaves into the vase.

2. Bake a cake in the Hexagon Ring Pan. Ice and place on serving tray. Pipe tube 10 bottom ball border. Pipe top border with tube 7 bulbs to form stylized tulips. See page 42 for technique. Pipe two balls between each flower. Add tube 6 balls down each corner and below tulips. Pipe tube 6 balls around hole in center of cake. Place tulip arrangement in hole. Serves twelve guests at a spring party.

Leprechauns are gnomes who live in Ireland

The next time you hear a little rustle in the grass, look close! It may be one of the little people! These jolly wee gentlemen dress always in green and their hair is invariably red. Their chief pleasure is visiting—telling old tales, dreaming up new ones and posing philosophical problems. Leprechaun women are passionate housekeepers and equally fond of talk. Since their get-togethers are held in the kitchen over cups of strong tea, they have never been seen by mortals. The children are known for their ruddy complexions and mischievous ways.

Pipe the leprechauns

The figure piping technique brings this pair to life as they sit on a log discussing the legendary pot of gold. This is the best icing to use.

WILTON PIPING ICING
  3 cups granulated sugar
  ⅔ cup water
  ¼ teaspoon cream of tartar
  4 tablespoons meringue powder
  ⅔ cup lukewarm water
  1¼ cups sifted confectioners' sugar

Cook the first three ingredients above to 236°F and set aside. Beat meringue with ⅔ cup lukewarm water until it peaks. Add confectioners' sugar slowly to meringue mixture, then beat at medium speed until blended. Now pour the cooked mixture into meringue mixture, wrap the bowl with towels wrung out of cold water to cool the icing while you are beating and continue beating at medium speed until peaks form. (Note: use a heavy-duty mixer.)

1. Make the pot by covering a 1″ ball of styrofoam (or marzipan) with marzipan (recipe page 159). Roll a long thin marzipan cylinder and attach around top of ball for rim, using egg white or piping gel for glue. Model three little legs and attach to ball. Cut gold coins from thinly rolled marzipan with tube 2A. Brush coins with corn syrup and sprinkle with edible glitter. Secure to pot with icing.

Roll a cylinder of marzipan about 1″ thick, 6″ long. Shape into a log and score with a modeling stick to resemble bark. Let harden about a day, set on wax paper and pipe leprechaun right on the log.

2. Hold tube 2A straight up and pipe a pointed pear shape about 2″ high for body. Insert a popsicle stick for support. Insert tube 11 into base of body and pipe a leg. Pipe second leg, then use tube 7 for shoes, pulling out to a point. Add a tube 2 string around ankle.

3. Insert tube 11 into top of body and pipe arms, then tube 2 cuffs and buttons. Pipe a tube 2 ball for hand and pull out fingers with same tube. Use tube 5 to circle top of body for collar.

4. Pipe tube 2 lines of icing on stick for neck. Use tube 2 for head. Pipe a long oval on back of popsicle stick for back of head. Pipe a bulb for forehead, two for cheeks and one for chin. Now pipe nose and two curves for eyebrows. Do eyes and mouth with piping gel and tube 1. Make a paper hat by cutting a wedge—one-third of a 3″ circle. Twirl into cone and tape. Set on head on a mound of icing, then add pointed tube 2 ears and tube 1 beard and hair.

Pipe the second leprechaun beside the first in a companionable pose. Allow to dry thoroughly.

Prepare the cake

Bake, fill and ice a two-layer oval cake. Pat top with a damp sponge and set on serving tray. Pipe a tube 6 ball border at base, tube 3 at top. Pipe stems on side with tube 4, then top with shamrocks piped with tube 104. Carefully remove log from wax paper and set on cake top. Add clumps of grass with tube 1 and set pot of gold beside cake. This little Gaelic treat serves twelve.

Quick & clever Easter cakes bring in springtime

Make the children jump for joy with an Easter cake as bright as the season. You'll have fun doing the decorating!

A bow-tied Easter egg
Tie a magnificent flowered egg cake with a ribbon bow. For a spring spectacular, garnish the tray with charming little sugar chicks!

1. Mold chicks with Easter Molds set and egg bases with half of a 3″ plastic Ball Mold. After bases have dried about one-half hour, score lines for jagged edge. Carefully remove edge pieces when scooping out center. Paint eyes and beaks on chicks with thinned royal icing. Pipe a mound of royal icing in base and place chick in it. Hold in place and fill base with jelly beans. Dry.

2. Bake a cake in the Egg Pan. Chill, trim off base to flatten, then fill and secure halves with toothpicks. Cut the egg in half the other way, across the width. Place cut sides down on cooling rack. Ice halves with buttercream, then cover with Quick Poured Fondant (recipe on page 159).

3. After fondant has set, attach the two halves of the egg with buttercream and more toothpicks. Place egg on serving tray. Cover seam with ribbon. Trim egg with tube 2 scallops and dot flowers. Attach a bow to top with icing. Set chicks, one for each child, around egg on tray. An adorable centerpiece that will serve twelve guests.

Two ducks on a pond
This little tableau is based on a separator plate, so it can be lifted off the cake and enjoyed all spring.

1. Pipe royal icing drop flowers with tubes 33, 131 and 225. Add tube 2 centers and dry.

2. Mold ducks using Popular Request molds. Dry, then put together with royal icing. Paint beaks with thinned royal icing and pipe eyes with tube 6. Attach ribbon necktie and bonnet strings. Make paper hat for boy duck and attach drop flowers to the girl duck's head for her bonnet.

3. Bake, fill and ice an 8″ x 4″ round, two-layer cake. Place on cake board. Pat icing with a clean, damp sponge for "grass". Ice top of a 6″ round separator plate and center on cake. Pipe tube 8 line of green icing around edge of plate, then fill with tinted piping gel for pond.

4. Pipe tube 4 stems on side of cake and add tube 65 leaves. Attach drop flowers on dots of icing. Pipe "grass" border around base of cake with tube 234. Cover top of cake up to pond with tube 234 "grass". Edge pond with flowers and pipe tube 65 leaves. Place ducks on pond, then display your spring creation to the children. Serves ten.

Figure piping brings Easter bunnies to life on a cake

Two big bunnies show off their colored eggs—little bunnies romp on the cake side. Create all these cunning creatures with the figure piping technique. (See page 58 for more figure piped trims.)

Pipe the big bunnies

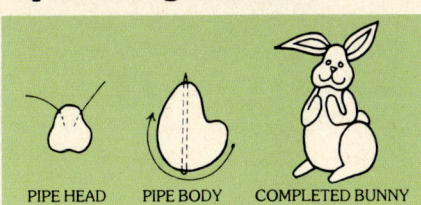

Pipe heads and bodies separately in royal icing on wax paper. Use tube 2A for both. Pipe a pear shape for head, keeping tip of tube buried in icing. Insert tube in side of head and squeeze for two plump cheeks. Insert two cloth-covered wires to support ears.

To pipe the body of upright bunny, begin at the back. Squeeze heavily, then pull the tube up and toward you, following the arrow in diagram. Insert toothpick for support. For body of crouching bunny, squeeze heavily, then move to front, decreasing pressure. When thoroughly dry, attach heads to bodies with icing. Pipe back legs, then front legs with tube 11. Pipe ears over the wires with tube 5. Pipe features and brush insides of the ears with tinted piping gel. Add ball-shaped tails with tube 12.

Figure pipe the Easter eggs in bright colors with tube 11. Keep the tip of the tube buried in the icing while piping, move up while decreasing pressure, stop pressure and pull away. Dry.

Pipe the tiny bunnies

The bunny cutter from the Party Cutter set is a guide in piping these little bunnies. Trace it on a stiff board and cover with wax paper. You will need 24.

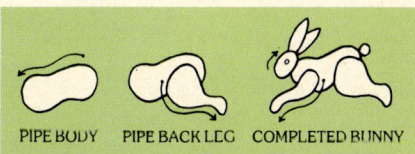

Using tube 6 and royal icing, pipe the body, beginning at the back and moving to the front. Add the back leg with the same tube, starting at the top and moving down. Pipe front leg with tube 3. Pipe head, ears and tail with the same tube. Add eye with tinted piping gel. Dry thoroughly.

Decorate the cake

Bake, fill and ice an 8" x 4" square, two-layer cake. Pipe bottom bulb border with tube 7, top bulb border with tube 4. Secure six tiny bunnies to each side of cake with dots of icing. Pipe a grassy patch on top of the cake with tube 234, then place big bunnies and eggs on top. Serve to twelve.

61

Fresh, flowery treats for springtime parties

Shamrock bouquets
May your dreams come true March 17!

1. Pipe royal icing shamrocks in advance. Pipe three heart-shaped leaves for each with tube 102. Cover lengths of florists' wire with icing by pushing the wire into a decorating bag fitted with tube 4. Squeeze bag while pulling out wire. Secure covered wires to eight shamrocks as stems.

2. Bake, fill and ice a 10" x 4" square, two-layer cake. Cut a piece of paper the same size as one side of cake, fold in thirds and cut a curve. Transfer this pattern to sides of cake. Outline the scallops with tube 2. Pipe tube 17 rosette base border. Mark a 5" circle on the top of the cake and outline with tube 2. Cover top of cake outside the circle with tube 17 stars, continuing down the sides of cake to the scallops. Pipe three tube 4 stems below each scallop and add a tube 2 bow. Secure shamrocks to stems with icing.

3. Insert a piece of styrofoam into Wishing Well and paint roof with thinned royal icing. Let icing set and then secure wishing well to top of cake with icing. Push stemmed shamrocks into styrofoam and add a sprinkling of shamrocks on the cake top. Serves 20.

Lilac time!
Decorate this dainty centerpiece for a spring luncheon or tea.

1. Pipe lilac blossoms as described on page 154.

2. Bake, fill and ice a 10" x 4" round, two-layer cake. Place on serving tray. Pipe tube 5 bottom bulb border. Divide side of tier into twelfths and drop a string guideline from point to point. Following the guideline, pipe tube 104 ruffled garlands and edge with tube 2 beading. Pipe a line of tube 1 dots above garlands and add a single lilac blossom at the intersections.

3. Divide top of cake into sixths. Pipe tube 4 top bulb border, then make a lilac spray at each division as described on page 154. Serves 14.

Blossoming petits fours
These dainty little treats are perfect on the sweet table at a spring wedding.

1. Pipe violets in advance following the directions on page 156.

2. For triangular petits fours, bake a single-layer sheet cake, 2" high, and cut into 2" squares. Cut squares in half diagonally. For round petits fours, bake a single-layer sheet cake, 1½" high, and cut with a 2" round cutter. For a deluxe touch, split the cake into two layers and fill before cutting the shapes. Ice each lightly with buttercream, then place on rack with pan beneath it. Cover with Quick Poured Fondant (page 159) and allow to harden.

3. Trim cakes with flowers. On triangular ones, pipe a long tube 70 leaf and tube 2 stems. Add lily of the valley blossoms. Pipe a tube 2 dot and pull out four tube 1 points. Trim round petits fours with violets and tube 70 leaves.

1920. *"The top candy people did pulled sugar work. This is what my dad did best. To learn the art of cake decorating, he would teach the old French and German pastry chefs how to pull sugar, and they in turn would show him various techniques of cake decorating."* —NORMAN WILTON

Cut-out parasols
Quick & clever

The bride-to-be will love this darling shower cake topped with parasols made of cake.

1. Pipe tube 131 drop flowers with tube 2 centers. Bake a 9" x 1" petal layer and a 9" x 13" x 4" two-layer sheet cake. Cut parasols from petal layer (see diagram below). Assemble on cake bases cut the

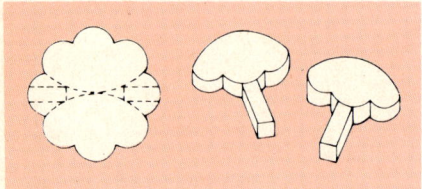

same size and shape. Ice parasols thinly. Outline sections with tube 4, then cover with tube 15 stars. Add tube 104 ruffle.

2. Set sheet cake on cake base, fill and ice, then place on cake board. Pipe tube 20 hearts and tube 2 message on side of cake. Pipe tube 20 bottom shell border with three upright shells at each corner. Pipe tube 16 shells around top edge and down corners. Place parasols on top of cake and trim with flowers and tube 65 leaves. Attach ribbon bow. Sheet cake serves 24, each parasol serves two.

Flower parasol
Quick & clever

An impressive little tier cake to decorate in a hurry, serve with pride.

1. Make the parasol. Ice a 4¼" Filigree Bell with royal icing. Paint an 8" long dowel rod with thinned icing. When dry, attach the dowel inside the bell with royal icing. Dry thoroughly. Pipe many drop flowers with tubes 26, 35 and 131. Add tube 2 centers and dry.

2. Bake a 6" x 2" single-layer round tier and a 10" x 4" two-layer round tier. Fill, ice and assemble on a serving tray. Pipe tube 8 bottom ball border on lower tier. Divide side of lower tier into twelfths. Drop a string guideline from point to point, then pipe a tube 8 zigzag garland following the guideline. Add tube 3 strings. Pipe tube 7 ball borders around top of lower tier and around top and bottom of upper tier.

3. Insert handle of parasol into top of cake. Attach flowers on dots of icing to tops of both tiers, to parasol and at the intersections of the garlands. Trim with tube 65 leaves. Cut a paper card and write tube 1 message. Attach a bow and the card to the parasol. Serves 17.

Paper parasols
Quick & clever

Give a shower cake a dainty Oriental air with brilliant Paper Parasols.

1. Bake 6" x 3" and 10" x 4" square, two-layer tiers. Set each on a cake base, fill and ice. Insert dowel rods, clipped level with top, in base tier. Assemble on cake board. On lower tier, pipe tube 2 message on side of tier, then pipe large comma-shaped shells with tube 20 for base border. Pipe tube 18 top shell border.

2. On upper tier, pipe tube 18 upright shells around bottom of tier. Pipe a pair of tube 2 strings connecting every other upright shell. Top each upright shell with a tube 17 star. Pipe tube 17 top shell border. Open the parasols and stick into cake. Serves 28 guests.

Pretty parasols

Honor the bride-to-be with one of these happy bridal shower cakes.

Each is full of good wishes for a bright future.

Spring things
Blossoms, singing birds and baby chicks say "Welcome spring!"

Fresh as flowers and bright as sunshine! Decorate one of these sweet cakes to center your Easter table—or to make any day a spring celebration.

Chicks in a nest
Figure piped chicks peek out from their nest on this joyous tulip cake. All trims are piped directly on the cake.

1. Bake 8″ x 4″ two-layer square and 6″ x 3″ two-layer round tiers. Fill, ice and assemble on a 10″ square cake board.
2. On bottom tier, pipe tube 7 bottom bulb border, tube 6 top bulb border. On side, pipe tube 4 stems, then pipe tube 7 tulips. Beginning at base of flower, pipe two outer petals first, then center petal. Use heavy pressure to begin, then reduce pressure gradually. Pipe tube 68 leaves on stemmed flowers.
3. On top tier, pipe tube 6 bottom bulb border, tube 5 top bulb border. On side of tier, pipe stems, tulips and leaves the same as on bottom tier.
4. For nest, mark a 4″ circle on top of cake and pipe with tube 233. Paint four miniature marshmallows with thinned icing and set in nest. Pipe chicks' heads on marshmallows with tube 10. Keep tip of tube buried in icing while squeezing for rounded shape. Stop pressure, then pull away. Pipe tube 65 beaks and tube 2 piping gel eyes. Pipe tube 7 eggs the same as on page 61. This happy treat serves 18.

The birds are back!
Quick & clever

Sparkling piping gel pipes the picture.

1. Pipe many royal icing drop flowers with tubes 33 and 131. Add tube 2 centers and dry.
2. Bake, fill and ice an 8″ x 4″ round, two-layer cake. Place on serving tray. Transfer *Celebrate! V* pattern to cake top, then outline with tube 2 and stiffened buttercream. Pipe tube 7 top bulb border. Secure drop flowers around base of cake with icing. Trim with tube 66 leaves.
3. Mix tinted piping gel with an equal amount of water. Place in parchment cone, cut tip and flow in within the piped outlines. Cake serves ten.

First sign of spring
One of the first flowers to announce spring are the dainty crocuses. Form them in golden gum paste to trim a bright cake.

1. Make a dozen gum paste crocuses and leaves using Flower Garden Cutter Set and instruction booklet. They're a quick flower to make! Bind flowers and leaves together with floral tape.
2. Bake a 10″ x 4″ round, two-layer cake. Fill and ice, then place on serving tray. We used a 5″ x 2″ round styrofoam dummy as upper tier to hold flowers. Ice with royal icing, pat with damp sponge and place on 5½″ separator plate. Edge base with tube 14 shells. This little garden can be lifted off the cake and saved for lasting spring decor. Set dummy tier on top of cake.
3. Divide side of 10″ tier into twelfths. At each division, pipe a tube 22 upright shell. Fill base border between them with tube 22 shells. Drop tube 14 strings between the upright shells and top them with tube 14 rosettes. Add tube 17 top shell border.
4. Arrange flowers in 5″ tier, pushing stems into styrofoam. Surround the garden with an Old Fashioned Fence, securing to cake with icing. Lift off garden before serving to 14 guests.

50 happy years of decorating

A cuddly teddy bear

He's a cute little way to welcome the new addition to the family.

1. In advance, pipe tube 225 drop flowers. Add tube 2 centers.

2. Bake the teddy bear in the small Panda Mold. Cover him with tube 14 stars for a fluffy look. Use tube 3 to pipe his eyes, nose and mouth. Secure him to the 5½" separator plate from the Round Mini-tier set with icing.

3. Bake, fill and ice an 8" x 4" square, two-layer cake. Place on a serving tray. Divide each side of cake into fourths and mark. Drop a tube 2 string guideline from point to point. Fill the area between the guideline strings and the base of the cake with tube 14 stars. Secure drop flowers to the sides of the cake with dots of icing, then trim them with tube 2 stems and leaves. Pipe tube 16 top shell border.

4. Center the separator plate, with the teddy bear on it, on top of the cake. Mark its position and remove. Insert three ¼" dowel rods down into the cake within this area to the cake board. Mark the spot where the top of the cake meets the dowel, then lift up and clip off so the dowels will be level with the top of the cake. Push them back down into the cake. These dowels are needed to support the teddy bear cake. Replace the separator plate on top of the cake and push down until it is level with the cake surface. Trim separator plate with flowers and tube 65 leaves.

5. Trim a Party Parasol with drop flowers and tube 65 leaves. Add a ribbon bow. Insert handle into teddy bear's paw. Attach a ribbon bow at his neck with a dab of icing. This adorable cake serves twelve. The mother-to-be will take home the teddy bear.

Sweet stuffed animals
Quick & clever

Create darling little "stuffed animal" baby toys with sugar molds to trim a welcoming cake. It's easy to do and really is sensational at the shower.

1. Mold two lions, horses and bunnies in the Animals Mold using the sugar mold recipe and technique on page 11. If you wish, add some edible glitter to the sugar mixture before molding the animals to give them sparkle. When dry, pipe details with tube 2.

2. Pipe a few tube 225 drop flowers and add tube 2 centers.

3. Bake, fill and ice a 12" x 4" two-layer hexagon cake. Place on serving tray. Pipe ruffled bottom border with tube 112. Secure sugar mold animals to sides of cake with icing, letting them rest on the serving tray. Pipe tube 112 ruffles down the corners of the cake, then add top ruffle border with the same tube. Lace a pair of Crystal-Clear Booties with ribbon, then attach them to the top of the cake with icing. Cut a paper card and pipe message on it with tube 2. Make a hole in one end of the card and insert a ribbon end through it. Attach drop flowers on dots of icing. Serve to 20 shower guests.

A bib for baby
Quick & clever

Trim this pretty "bib" cake with a cute bunny holding a balloon.

1. Bake a 9" x 13" x 2" single-layer sheet cake and round off the corners slightly. Ice the cake and place it on a ruffle-edged cake board.

2. Transfer *Celebrate! V* bunny pattern to cake top. Mark a circle above it at the edge of the cake with a 4" round cutter. Pipe bunny and balloon with tube 13 stars and add details with tube 3.

3. Pipe tube 16 zigzag bottom border and trim with tube 3 dots. Around top edge of cake, pipe tube 104 ruffle, then tube 16 zigzag and trim with tube 3 dots. Pipe tube 16 zigzag around marked circle up to top border and trim with tube 3 dots. Pipe tube 3 message. Add a ribbon bow and serve to twelve party guests.

Baby talk

Welcome the new arrival and congratulate the happy parents

Honor the bride-to-be with this Quick & clever shower cake

Surprise her at the shower with this darling parasol cake. It's quick to make, easy to serve—she'll love it!

1. Bake a 9″ x 13″ x 4″ two-layer sheet cake. Set on cake base, fill and ice, then place on a foil-covered cake board. Pipe tube 16 zigzag base border, tube 14 zigzag top border.

2. Divide the area on top of the cake (within space for top border) into fourths on the short sides and into sixths on the long sides. Connect the divisions and mark the lines in the icing with edge of light cardboard. Pipe the lines with tube 14 zigzags.

3. Pipe a tube 2 handle in each square, then pipe parasol top with four tube 362 shells. Make center shells first, then two outer shells. Add a tube 2 dot at top and bow on handle. Pipe message with the same tube. Cut along the piped lines to serve to 24 guests.

IT'S EASTER! *Shown on page 55*

Make this spectacular Easter centerpiece cake to thrill young and old alike!

1. Pipe drop flowers using tubes 33, 131 and 191. Add tube 2 centers.

2. Make bunny. Bake two half-eggs in Egg Minicake Pan. Put them together with icing, fasten with toothpicks and trim the large end so it will stand up. Ice with buttercream. Insert a toothpick into each of two whole marshmallows and two half-marshmallows. Pour Quick Poured Fondant (recipe on page 159) over egg and dip marshmallows into the fondant. Let harden.

Using egg for body, push toothpicks on whole marshmallows in for feet, half marshmallows for arms. Fill crevices with icing. Insert a toothpick into a whole marshmallow and push into body for head. Cover head with tube 13 stars, piping star-on-star to build out cheeks. Cut paper ears (use *Celebrate!* V pattern or your own), sandwiching a toothpick between two pieces of paper for each ear so part of toothpick extends out. Insert the toothpicks into the head and pipe over the ears with tube 13 stars. Add features with tube 2. Whiskers are pieces of iced spaghetti. Pipe trims on suit with tubes 13 and 2.

3. Make basket. Bake a Small Wonder Mold. Trim off small end for base. Set on small cake circle cut to fit, ice. Pat large end with a damp sponge. Pipe tube 13 basket weave on sides. Secure bunny to top of basket with icing and trim with drop flowers.

4. Bake eight half-eggs in Egg Minicake Pan. Ice with buttercream, then cover with Quick Poured Fondant. When fondant hardens, trim eggs with tubes 2, 44, 101 and drop flowers.

5. Bake, fill and ice a 12″ x 4″ two-layer petal cake. Place on cake board. Pat top of cake with a damp sponge for grassy effect. Pipe tube 16 base shell border and tube 13 top shell border. Pipe tube 4 stems and tube 66 leaves on side, then add drop flowers. Secure bunny on basket and eggs to cake top with icing as shown. Petal cake serves 26, two half-eggs make one serving. You'll want to save the bunny for a few days. Icing keeps it fresh.

Celebrate!

THE MERRY MONTHS OF MAY AND JUNE

Golden day.
Decorating directions, page 76.

Romantic cakes

Romance is always in season, but May and June are the months that give decorators the most frequent opportunities to express the theme of love.

At Wilton, the bridal cake has been the crowning glory of the decorator's art for 50 years. In this issue we present a collection of magnificent wedding creations—some very modern, others adorned with graceful techniques of decades past that are just as beautiful today as they were then.

If you would like to view a much larger portfolio of wedding cakes, we are proud to announce a new book, also published in honor of our jubilee year, *Beautiful Bridal Cakes the Wilton Way.* In it are 80 all-new cakes, each clearly described, to inspire you to create your own romantic masterpieces.

Rose lace

A modern masterpiece with the new-again look of glossy poured fondant and a traditional cascade of beautiful roses. The rich chocolate groom's cake sets off the snowy bridal tiers and displays his initials and a similar cascade.

The Jubilee Roses were created just for *Celebrate! V* to celebrate the golden jubilee of Wilton Enterprises. See them also on our cover cake and on the graduation cake on page 93. Page 153 shows how to pipe them.

1. Make about 30 Golden Jubilee Roses in advance with royal icing using tubes 104 and 126. Pipe tube 67 leaves on wires and when dry, bind into clusters of three with floral tape. (See page 157 for instructions.)

2. Bake 14" x 4", 10" x 4" and 6" x 3½" two-layer round tiers. Fill and ice each tier smoothly with buttercream. Insert a circle of ¼" dowels clipped off level with top into two lower tiers. Place tiers on racks with pans beneath them. Cover with Quick Poured Fondant using recipe and pouring instructions on page 159. Let fondant harden, then assemble cake on an 18" foil-covered cake board. Pipe tube 5 bulb border around the base of each tier.

3. Reproduce the lace on the bridal gown for the lovely trim, or use *Celebrate! V* pattern. Trace pattern onto parchment paper. Transfer to edges of tiers by pricking holes in the fondant with a pin. Evenly space four designs on bottom tier, four on middle tier and two on top tier. Outline the design with tube 1 and Color Flow icing straight from the batch. Thin down the icing for flowing in until it is the consistency of thick honey. Flow into the areas of the pattern using a parchment cone with a tiny hole cut in the tip.

4. Insert Stairsteps into sides of tiers to create a curving stairway from the front of the bottom tier to the back of the top tier. This makes a convenient base for the Jubilee Rose cascade, easily removed at serving time. Secure roses and leaves to Stairsteps with mounds of royal icing. Attach Kissing Lovebirds to top tier and trim base with a rose and some leaves. Two lower tiers serve 140, top tier 16.

Salute the Groom

1. Make about 15 Jubilee Roses and leaves in advance the same as for the wedding cake. Pipe royal icing spikes on the backs of three roses.

2. Bake a 10" x 4" round, two-layer cake. Fill and ice with a smooth coat of chocolate buttercream. Place on rack and cover with Chocolate Quick Poured Fondant (recipe on page 159). When fondant has hardened, transfer to serving tray.

3. Trace initials onto cake top by pricking holes in fondant with a pin. Patterns are in *Celebrate! V Pattern Book.* Pipe letters with tube 1 and Color Flow icing straight from the batch. Thin the icing and flow in the areas of the letters. Secure roses and leaves to cake on mounds of icing. Serves 1" x 2" pieces to 48 guests.

1929. *"During the depression my dad started out teaching cake decorating classes. That was the start of Wilton Enterprises. At the same time, he also taught students individually. He charged $25 a lesson. That was a lot of money."* —NORMAN WILTON

Bridal bells.
Decorating directions, page 76.

Golden dawn. Decorating directions on page 77.

50
A trio of glowing bridal cakes created to honor Wilton's Jubilee year

Norman Wilton decorated these outstanding wedding cakes especially for this Jubilee edition of *Celebrate!*. Each is covered in rolled fondant. This satiny surface is a perfect background for the graceful trims—reminiscent of past styles of decorating.

Golden day *shown on page 71*

An important cake for a once-in-a-lifetime celebration.

1. Make royal icing flowers in advance—eight tube 104 roses and many sweet peas (page 42 tells how).
2. Bake two-layer round tiers—12", 10" and 6"—using a firm pound cake batter. Fill layers, then cover with marzipan and rolled fondant as described on page 29. Insert dowel rods, clipped level with top, in two lower tiers. Assemble on a 16" cake board, using 8" separator plates and 5" Grecian pillars with Snap-On Filigree.
3. On base tier, pipe tube 32 bottom star border. Trim with tube 4 string. Divide top edge of tier into eighths, then drop string guidelines. Pipe tube 18 "e" motion garlands and top with double tube 4 strings.
4. Pipe tube 18 reverse shell bottom border on middle tier. Using garlands on tier below as guide, divide top edge of tier into sixteenths. Drop string guidelines and pipe circling "e" motion garlands with tube 14. Trim with tube 4 strings and bows. On top of tier, pipe scallops with tube 3 and zigzag motion. Edge separator plate with tube 3.

Pipe tube 32 stars around base of top tier and trim with tube 4 string.

5. Spray flowers on Petite Spring Song ornament with yellow food color using an air brush. Secure ornament to top of cake with icing. Divide side of top tier into sixths, then make cascades of sweet peas at the divisions. Attach flowers on dots of icing.

Trim Kneeling Cherub Fountain with sweet peas and secure between pillars. Add Mediterranean Cupids at edge of lower separator plate. Attach flowers as pictured and trim with tube 65 leaves. Attach a rose at the bottom border beneath each garland and trim each with tube 67 leaves. Two lower tiers serve 116, top tier serves 16.

Golden Day

Bridal Bells *shown on page 74*

A lavishly trimmed bridal masterpiece accented with golden roses and matching wild roses. Pipe all the flowers in royal icing in advance, using tubes 104 and 127 for the roses, and tube 103 for wild roses. Pipe royal icing spikes on backs of 36 roses.

1. Make between-tiers ornament. Invert a small paper cup, cover with royal icing and then attach tube 104 roses all over the cup for a flower mound. For the top ornament, glue wild roses around the plate and heart frame of Bridal Bells ornament.
2. Bake the round tiers, 16", 12" and 8", each two layers. Use a firm pound cake recipe. Fill the layers and cover with rolled fondant as described on page 29. Insert dowel rods, clipped level with top, in two lower tiers then assemble the cake on a 20" cake board with 8" separator plates, 5" Grecian pillars and Snap-On Filigree. Before placing top tier in position, set prepared flower mound within the pillars.
3. Decorate base tier. First pipe tube 4B stars all around the base and drop a tube 4 string around each star. Divide top edge of tier into twelfths and drop string guidelines for garlands. Following guidelines, first pipe a fluted edge on the garlands using tube 102 and an up-and-down motion. Now pipe the garlands with tube 6, using light pressure at ends, heavy pressure in centers of garlands. Drop tube 4 strings below garlands, double tube 3 strings above. On top of tier, pipe scallops with tube 4, using back-and-forth motion. Finish top edge with tube 17 reverse shells.
4. Decorate middle tier. Pipe puffy, tube 4B shells around base and trim with tube 3 dropped strings. Divide top edge of tier into twelfths and drop string guidelines about 2" deep. Pipe garland with tube 16 and up-and-down motion, squeezing lightly at ends of garlands, heavily in center. Add double tube 3 strings. On top of tier, pipe tube 4 curves above each garland and fill in with tube 3 lattice. Edge lattice with tube 3 bulbs and complete top border with tube 16 reverse shells.
5. Decorate top tier. The graceful base border is unusual in that it drops below the tier edge. Divide into fourteenths, mark about 1" up from base and drop strings for guidelines. Pipe tube 13 garlands. With tube 3, make long "S" curves, from beginning of one garland

Bridal Bells

to its end, and up over to third garland on side of tier. Drape a second tube 3 string over garlands and cover curves above with tube 3 in back-and-forth movement. Make full garlands on top edge of tier with tube 13, using garlands below as guide. Trim with tube 3 string and use same tube to connect garlands on top of tier with scallops, using back-and-forth motion.

Now do the finishing touches. Secure top ornament and cover base with roses, attaching with royal icing. Attach a wild rose between each base garland on top tier. Secure Mediterranean Cupids to top of middle tier and add roses. Circle garlands on side of tier with wild roses and make rose cascades on base tier. Trim roses with tube 66 leaves. Two lower tiers serve 186, top tier serves 30.

Golden Dawn shown on page 75
Airy daisies and yellow wild roses trim this dainty little masterpiece. Make the royal icing flowers in advance using tube 103 with tube 5 centers for the daisies, tube 103 with tube 1 centers for the wild roses. Dry all within curves.

1. Bake two-layer round tiers—14" x 4" and 8" x 3". Fill, then cover with rolled fondant tinted a sunshine yellow (page 29). Assemble on cake board with Harvest Cherub separator set. Divide side of 14" tier in twelfths and mark 2" up on cake side. Divide side on 8" tier in twelfths and mark ¾" up on cake side.

2. Decorate base tier. Make a star drop base border with tube 17 and trim with tube 3 loops. Drop string guidelines from marks on tier side and pipe tube 5 circular motion garlands. Top with double tube 3 strings and "Italian" bows. On top edge of tier, drop string guidelines, lining up with garlands below. Pipe circular motion tube 16 garlands, then trim with double tube 3 strings. Mark shallow scallops on the tier top to connect each garland, then fill in the space between scallops and separator plate with tube 1 cornelli. Edge plate with tube 4 bulbs and outline scallops with same tube and back-and-forth movements.

3. On top tier, drop string guidelines from marks on tier side. Pipe tube 4 garlands over the guidelines in tight zigzags. Drop tube 3 strings over garlands. From top edge of tier, drop string guidelines for garlands, lining up with garlands below. With tube 4, connect garlands on top of the tier in scallops. Fill in space between scallops and guidelines with tube 1 cornelli. Pipe gar-

Golden Dawn

lands over guidelines and scallops with tube 3 zigzags. Drape lower garland with double tube 3 strings.

Attach Adoration ornament within pillars and Petite Heavenly Bells ornament on top of cake. Circle the seated cherubs with wild roses, then trim ornaments and tiers with wild roses and daisies. Lower tier of this charming centerpiece serves 92, upper tier serves 30.

White lace
Decorating directions on page 80

Rosy dream
Decorating directions on page 80

White lace shown on page 78

Frilly lace and delicate piping make this a bride's dream cake! All patterns are in *Celebrate! V Pattern Book*.

1. Make lace pieces with royal icing and tube 1s. You need 80 large and 72 smaller pieces (see page 54).

Pipe royal icing drop flowers using tubes 33, 224 and 225.

2. For bottom tier, bake a 16" base bevel layer, two 12" x 1½" round layers and a 12" top bevel layer. Fill between base bevel and one 12" layer, then fill between other 12" layer and top bevel. Assemble as two tiers on a 20" cake board, inserting dowels for support into both tiers and placing a 10" separator plate between them. Ice smoothly.

For top tier, bake an 8" top bevel layer and an 8" x 2" layer. Fill and ice. Assemble tiers with 8" round separator plates and 5" Corinthian pillars.

3. Decorate bottom tier. Using pillars as guide, transfer large heart pattern to tier side. Outline with tube 2 beading, then pipe scallops and dots with same tube. Edge separator plate with tube 7 bulbs. Trace scroll pattern between hearts. Pipe with tube 5, then over-pipe with tubes 4, 2 and 2. Dry, then paint scrolls with thinned icing. Add tube 4 dots above scroll design. Pipe tube 7 bottom ball border, tube 6 ball border below scrolls, tube 4 beading between hearts at lower edge of top bevel and tube 5 beading around top edge of tier. Pipe tube 2 dots on base bevel. Trim with flowers and tube 65 leaves.

4. Decorate top tier. Divide side of tier at bevel into eighths. Drop string guidelines, then pipe with tube 2 beading. Pipe tube 5 top border and add tube 2 dots. At bottom edge of tier, mark scroll pattern. Pipe with tube 5, then over-pipe with tubes 4, 2 and 2. Mark a 3½" circle on top of tier. Outline with tube 3 and flow in thinned blue icing. Pipe tube 4 beading around edge. Secure Kneeling Cherub Fountain between pillars, Musical Trio to top of tier. Trim with flowers and leaves.

Now add lace pieces to both tiers, starting with smaller pieces and top tier. Page 54 gives method. Cut bottom tier as two tiers. Bottom tier serves 136, top tier serves 30.

To carry, remove top tier with pillars and attach to an 8" separator plate to prevent bottom trim from getting broken. Reassemble cake at reception.

Rosy dream shown on page 79

Trim rosy tiers with pink impatiens and see how pretty a petite cake can be! The realistic flowers are quickly made from gum paste.

1. Make many impatiens and leaves from gum paste using Flower Garden Cutter Set and instruction booklet. Bind most of the flowers and leaves together in small clusters.

2. Bake 12" x 4" square and 8" x 3" round, two-layer tiers. Fill and ice tiers smoothly. Mark square tier with an 8" cake circle and insert dowel rods, clipped level with top, within it. Assemble on 16" cake board using 8" separator plates and 5" Corinthian pillars.

3. Decorate bottom tier. Pipe tube 22 shells around base, then frame with tube 14 zigzags on cake board. Between shells, pipe tube 14 stars. Edge separator plate with tube 6. Using *Celebrate! V* pattern, mark hearts on tier. Outline with tube 13 curved shells. Pipe tube 16 reverse shell top border.

4. Decorate top tier. Pipe tube 15 bottom shell border. Transfer heart pattern to front and back of tier. Outline with tube 13 curved shells. Pipe tube 13 reverse shell top border.

5. Secure impatiens to tiers as pictured. Secure Angel Fountain between pillars with icing. Remove flowers from Enchantment ornament. Secure to cake, then trim ornaments with impatiens. Lower tier serves 72, top tier serves 30.

Ruffled petunia shown at right

A classically beautiful cake, all in white, for a formal wedding reception.

1. Make royal icing petunias as directed on page 85. You need six dozen. Mount twelve on wire stems. Pipe a tube 5 spike on back of eight.

2. Bake 16" x 4", 12" x 4" and 8" x 3" two-layer round tiers. Fill, ice and insert supporting dowel rods in two lower tiers. Assemble on a 20" cake board using 12" separator plates and 7½" Corinthian pillars.

3. Pipe tube 22 bottom shell border and tube 20 top shell border on base tier. Divide side of tier into twenty-fourths. Drop string guidelines for garlands, four across front of cake, then skipping a mark for large garland below pillar. Continue around side. Pipe tube 18 zigzag garlands. Trim with tube 3 strings, tube 17 fleurs-de-lis and stars. Edge separator plate with tube 17.

4. On middle tier, pipe tube 20 bottom shell border and tube 18 top shell border. Divide side of tier into twelfths, drop guidelines, then pipe tube 18 zigzag garlands. Add tube 3 strings, tube 17 fleurs-de-lis and rosettes.

5. Pipe tube 18 shell borders on top tier. Divide side into eighths, drop guidelines and pipe tube 18 zigzag garlands. Trim with tube 3 strings and tube 17 rosettes. Secure Kissing Lovebirds ornament between pillars, then trim cake with petunias, securing them on mounds of icing and pushing spiked flowers into side of cake. Insert a Flower Spike into top of cake and arrange stemmed petunias in it. Surround with more flowers. Pipe tube 69 leaves. Two lower tiers serve 186, top tier serves 30.

Ruffled petunia
Decorating directions at left

This romantic, ribboned bridal cake tells love's story with beautifully piped flowers. The announcement cake is a pretty preview.

The bridal cake

The flowers trimming this lovely cake hold a message of good wishes for the bridal couple—yellow lilies for love's gaiety, bridal roses for happy love, forget-me-nots for true love.

1. Make royal icing flowers in advance. For lilies, press foil into a 1⅝″ lily nail. With tube 75, pipe a long petal, pulling out over edge of nail into a point. Pipe two more petals spaced evenly around nail. Pipe three more petals between the first three, overlapping slightly. Add tube 14 green star in center and push in artificial stamens.

Pipe roses with tubes 103 and 104. Make forget-me-nots with tube 101. Pipe a few tube 225 drop flowers. Pipe a tube 5 spike on backs of half the lilies and on eight of the large roses. (See page 157).

2. Make heart-shaped box using Heart Minicake pan and sugar mold recipe on page 11. Add some edible glitter to the sugar mixture for sparkle. Mold two hearts, hollow out carefully and dry thoroughly. Secure flowers in one heart with icing. Trim with tube 66 leaves. Pipe tube 2 beading around edges of hearts, then assemble with royal icing, propping box open with cotton until dry. Attach a ribbon bow with icing.

3. Bake 16″ x 4″, 12″ x 4″ and 8″ x 3″ round, two-layer tiers and a 6″ x 3″ two-layer heart tier. Fill, ice and assemble on a 20″ ruffle-edged cake board using 9″ round separator plates and 5″ Corinthian pillars. Insert dowel rods in three lower tiers, clipped off level with top of tiers.

4. On bottom tier, pipe tube 10 bottom and tube 7 top bulb borders. Divide side of tier into sixteenths. Drop a string guideline from point to point, then pipe over guideline with tube 7 zigzag garland. Trim the garlands with tube 3 strings and hearts.

On 12″ tier, pipe tube 8 bottom, tube 7 top bulb borders. Edge separator plate with tube 7. Pipe hearts on tier side with tube 5, trim with tube 3.

On 8″ tier, pipe tube 7 bottom, tube 6 top bulb borders. Divide side of tier into tenths. Drop a string guideline from point to point, then pipe tube 7 zigzag garland over guideline. Trim garland with tube 3 strings and hearts. Edge top tier with tube 6 bulb borders.

5. Trim standing cherub ornament with drop flowers and attach to cake top. Secure flowers to top and second tiers with icing. Pipe a tube 104 bow. Secure heart box between pillars with icing, then trim second and bottom tiers with flowers. Add tube 104 ribbon bows. Trim all flowers with tube 66 leaves. This masterpiece cake serves 216, not including the 12-serving top tier.

The announcement cake

This happy, flowery cake is a preview of the wedding cake to come.

1. Make yellow lilies, roses and forget-me-nots the same as for the wedding cake. Pipe tube 5 spikes on the backs of a few lilies and roses.

2. Bake 10″ x 4″ round, two-layer cake. Fill, ice and place on serving tray. Pipe tube 10 bottom, tube 7 top bulb borders. Pipe tube 104 ribbons and bow, tube 2 message. Secure flowers with dots of icing. Serve to 14 guests.

Mother's day

Hearts and flowers trim sweet feminine cakes designed for her pleasure on Mother's day!

Bouquets of carnations

Deck her cake with the fluffy pink flowers that are the symbol of Mother's day.

1. Make the royal icing carnations in advance. Pipe them with stiffened icing to create the characteristic broken petal effect. Stripe decorating bag with light pink icing, then fill with dark pink icing. Touch tube 104 to the center of number 7 flower nail. Move out about 1⅛", jiggling hand gently and lifting slightly as you reach petal tip. Curve around, return to center of nail and stop pressure. Repeat for a circle of ruffled petals. Pipe another circle of petals on top of the first, lifting them a bit more upright. Add a third circle of petals, shorter and still more upright. Fill center with vertical petals. You will need about twelve carnations.

2. Bake a 9" oval, two-layer cake. Fill, ice and place on serving tray. Pipe tube 32 base shell border and trim shells with tube 4 dots. For top border, pipe a tube 5 string around the top edge of the cake. Pipe a row of tube 16 shells along each side of the string. Pipe a third row of shells on top of the string. Add tube 4 dots between shells on either side of the center row.

3. Divide side of cake into sixteenths. Pipe a tube 2 string from point to point, then top the intersections with dots. Pipe tube 2 lettering on top of cake and add scallops and dots beneath it with the same tube. Attach carnations at each end of the cake on the serving tray with icing. Trim with tube 67 leaves. Serves twelve guests.

Ruffled petunias in a wreath

A dainty cake trimmed with petunias and forget-me-nots that has a look reminiscent of yesteryear. It's a sweet tribute on Mother's day.

1. Make royal icing flowers in advance. For petunias, line a 1⅝" lily nail with foil, then with the narrow end of tube 102 up, start piping royal icing deep inside nail. Move up to outer edge as you turn nail, jiggling hand slightly for ruffled petals, then return to starting point. Repeat for a total of five petals. Pipe a tube 14 green star in center and insert a few artifical stamens. Dry, then peel off foil and pipe a tube 6 royal icing spike on the back of each petunia. Dry. For forget-me-nots, hold tube 101 at a 45° angle to the flower nail. Move out about ⅜" from center, curve around and return, letting turn of nail form petals. Pipe center dot with tube 1.

2. Bake one layer in the 8" top bevel pan and one 8" x 2" round layer. Attach to cake circle, fill between the layers and ice with buttercream. Place on a cooling rack with a pan underneath, then cover with poured fondant (recipe on page 159). When fondant has hardened, transfer cake to a serving tray. For bottom border, pipe tube 32 shells and trim the base of each with a tube 14 zigzag. Pipe a tube 17 star between the tops of the shells.

3. Pipe "Mother" on top with tube 2. Secure flowers around edge of top bevel. Push spikes on petunias through a mound of icing and into the cake. Fill in with forget-me-nots on dots of icing. Trim with tube 67 leaves. Add a ribbon bow. Serves ten.

A picture of love

Rolled fondant, with its satin finish, covers this lovely Mother's day cake. A pierced lift-off plaque of Color Flow gives an intriguing play of light and shadow, smaller motifs trim the sides. It's a cake that expresses a lot of love.

1. Make Color Flow pieces. Tape *Celebrate! V* pattern for plaque to a flat surface, patterns for six side motifs to a 10" curved surface. Cover with wax paper. Outline plaque and side motifs with tube 2 and Color Flow icing straight from the batch. Dry, then flow in the areas with thinned Color Flow icing using a cut cone. Dry thoroughly.

2. Bake a 10" x 3" round, two-layer cake. Fill the layers and secure to a cake circle the same size as the cake. Using the recipes for marzipan and rolled fondant on page 159, cover the cake as described on page 29. Transfer cake to a foil-covered cake board.

3. Pipe tube 10 bottom ball border. Carefully peel wax paper from backs of Color Flow pieces. Divide side of cake into sixths, then attach a Color Flow motif at each division with icing. Secure plaque to top of cake on sugar cubes with dots of icing. Lift off the plaque before serving and present it to Mother. It's pretty enough to frame! Cake serves 14.

50 happy years of decorating

A replica of a cake for Mother's day, created many years ago.

Perhaps you remember seeing this cake in *Modern Cake Decorating*. Norman Wilton re-created it for *Celebrate! V*—it's just as pretty today.

A graceful cake for Mother

Make all the royal icing flowers in advance and dry. Pipe roses with tubes 102 and 103, daisies with tube 103 petals and tube 5 centers, a few tube 103 wild roses, and daffodils with tube 103 petals and tube 3 centers. (See page 57.) Pipe royal icing spikes on the backs of six roses and on one or two daffodils (page 157).

1. Bake a 12″ two-layer cake. Fill and ice smoothly and place on serving tray. Pipe the script on the cake top with tube 1 and a mixture of equal parts of piping gel and royal icing. Position it a little forward of center front. For the decorative build-up on the letters, pause slightly and make a slight back-and-forth movement for a rippled effect.

2. Divide cake side into sixteenths and mark with dots of icing about 2″ up from base. Pipe base star drop border with tube 21 and trim with tube 3 string. Drop string guidelines for garlands from marks. Pipe tube 5 garlands with a back-and-forth movement, light pressure at ends of garlands, heavy in center. Drop double tube 3 strings, then pipe "Italian" bows in a figure eight motion and add streamers.

From top edge of cake, drop string guidelines for garlands, positioning so center of curve is directly above end points of garlands below. Pipe garlands with tube 16 zigzags, then over-pipe with same tube and motion. Now pipe tube 3 lattice with thinned icing from top edge of cake to garland. Mark scallops on top of cake to connect points of garlands. Pipe scallops with tube 3 and back-and-forth movement, then edge scallops with same tube, light pressure.

3. Spatula stripe a decorating cone fitted with tube 4 with beige icing and fill with brown icing. Pipe a group of curved stems, adding a little twirl at end of each. Pipe a crescent of icing on cake top, starting where stems join. Use any large tube. Now arrange flowers on and around crescent, tilting each on a mound of icing. Make a cascade down side of cake by pushing in spiked flowers on icing mounds.

Spatula stripe a decorating cone fitted with tube 66 with brown icing, then fill with thinned green icing for leaves. Pipe the leaves and your Mother's day tribute is complete. Serves 22.

Pansies adorn Father's cake

Flowers can be used very effectively on a man's cake, too. These richly colored blossoms set off a tailored cake.

1. Make royal icing pansies in advance following the instructions on page 156. Pipe a tube 5 spike on the backs of a dozen of the flowers.

2. Bake, fill and ice a 10″ x 4″ round, two-layer cake. Place on serving tray. Divide side of cake into fourths and mark lightly 2″ up from base. Now pipe arched side border with tube 17. ½″ from mark, pipe a 2″ vertical line. 1½″ away, pipe a second line. Join the two lines with curved shells to form arch, and pipe an upright shell and star where they meet. Pipe a second arch within division the same as the first. Divide space between the two arches in half and mark 1½″ up from base. Drop double strings to connect as picture shows and top ends of string with rosettes. Repeat design in other divisions.

3. Pipe tube 17 rosettes around the base of the cake, tube 16 shells around top. Pipe tube 2 message on top of cake. On top edge of cake, form four clusters of pansies, tilting each on an icing mound. Push in spiked flowers on side of cake on mounds of icing. Trim with tube 66 leaves. Serves 14.

1946. *"We taught classes in our dining room in the apartment on Parnell Avenue. I can recall the students walking down the street, carrying their suitcases, looking all around. I'd run out and ask, 'Are you looking for the Wilton School? It's here in the house.' They would look very perturbed, but once they took the course, they were delighted with it. How hard we worked with them!"*—NORMAN WILTON

Dad's a gardener

Want to decorate a cake for a gardener that will really thrill him? Just wheel in this cart of vegetables. First get out your Flower Cart and spray it a verdant green. (Leave tray white.)

Model the vegetables
These marzipan mimics are just as delicious as the real thing.

1. Make a recipe of marzipan (page 159), divide into portions and tint. Leave a little untinted for potatoes. For uniform size, roll the tinted marzipan into cylinders on a board dusted with confectioners' sugar. Roll cylinders into 1½" diameter for large tomatoes, potatoes and green peppers, 1" diameter for beets and ¾" diameter for cherry tomatoes and red peppers.

2. Working with one color at a time, slice off pieces from the cylinders equal to the diameter. Roll into shape between your palms, then use a wooden modeling stick to make grooves and depressions. Roll untinted marzipan into rough ovals for potatoes, make eyes with a stick, moisten with a damp cloth and roll in sifted cocoa. Roll carrots into long narrow cylinders, point the ends and score with a stick. Model peppers, then cut one in half and shape with your fingers. The seeds are tiny balls of untinted marzipan, flattened. Model most leaves by hand from small balls of marzipan. Roll out marzipan ⅛" thick on a board dusted with confectioners' sugar and cut more leaves with the Rose Leaf Cutter from the Flower Garden set. Hand-model stems and attach to vegetables with egg white or piping gel. Dry all the vegetables 24 hours, then glaze (see page 159).

Prepare the cake
Bake a two-layer cake in oval pans, fill, ice and place on tray that comes with the Flower Cart. Cover the sides with tube 2B and pipe tube 15 borders—shell at base, reverse shell at top. Set the cake on the Flower Cart and carefully arrange vegetables. Fill in with a few cut leaves. Print message on a paper card with tube 2, attach to handle with a fluffy bow and present to a delighted Dad. Serves twelve.

Mom loves flowers

This charming tribute to Mother features a perky little flower girl standing in a field of California poppies. First spray a Flower Cart a sunny yellow, then make the flowers from gum paste according to directions on page 94. This new flower goes together quickly.

Make the gum paste girl
1. Use the five-year-old molds from the Wilton People Mold set and accompanying instruction booklet. When basic figure is dry, cut ¼" strips from thinly rolled gum paste and wrap around feet for shoes, trimming excess at back. Use egg white as glue.
2. To make bodice, cut a 1½" x 3" strip from thinly rolled gum paste. Wrap around figure and trim and smooth at neck, armholes, back and lower edge. Her skirt consists of four petals cut with the Small Violet Leaf cutter from the Flower Garden set. Cut ¼" off pointed end and roll rounded edge of leaf with modeling stick 4 to slightly ruffle. Attach a petal to front of figure just below bodice, then back, then one on either side. Roll a string of gum paste and attach to cover waistline seam.
3. Her hat is a full-size poppy dried in a lily nail (page 94). Omit stamens and add a tiny string for stem. Make up the face as directed in booklet, then pipe hair with tubes 13 and 1. Set hat on head while hair is wet. Pipe tube 1s laces on shoes. Attach arms to figure and secure a little bouquet of stemmed tiny poppies to hands. Cover a plate from Petite Heart Base with rolled gum paste, dry and edge with tube 1. Attach dried figure to plate by brushing tiny balls of gum paste with egg white and pressing to bottoms of feet. Brush again and set figure on plate.

Prepare the cake
Bake, fill and ice a two-layer oval cake. Set on Flower Cart tray, cover sides with tube 2B, edge with tube 16 shells, and letter a paper card with tube 2. Attach flower girl on plate to top of cake with icing, then arrange poppies, stemmed and unstemmed, around girl. Push spiked poppies into sides of cake and pipe tube 2 thread-like leaves. Set cake on cart and tie a ribbon bow to handle. Mother will be overwhelmed! This flowery treat serves twelve.

No words are needed to express your love for Dad

—just one of these kingly cakes!

Royal crown

Here's a real extravaganza to present to Father on his day—he'll be amazed and delighted! Rich pound cake, chocolate fondant and marzipan make it taste as good as it looks. Fondant and marzipan recipes are on page 159.

1. Bake a cake in the Turk's Head Mold and a single-layer 2″ high cake in an 8″ round pan. Set the round cake on an 8″ cake circle and ice in buttercream. Insert a circle of ¼″ dowels, clipped off level with top. Attach an 8″ cake circle to Turk's Head, ice thinly with buttercream, then cover with fondant. Assemble the cake on serving tray.

2. Make a recipe of gold-tinted marzipan, roll out, and cut a strip 2″ by about 24″. Brush side of round cake with piping gel and wrap strip around side of cake to bring it flush with Turk's Head. Cut another strip of marzipan 2½″ wide by about 26″ and wrap cake again, attaching with piping gel and trimming seam to butt neatly. Mark a line with a pin 1½″ from base on strip.

Cut twelve each of large ivy and lily leaves from marzipan using Flower Garden cutters. Dry on a 9″ curve. Cut two marzipan crosses following *Celebrate! V* pattern. Brush one with piping gel, lay a popsicle stick on it, end protruding, and cover with second cross. Dry flat.

3. Attach leaf shapes to marzipan strip on cake with piping gel as picture shows. Trim with royal icing. Starting at top center of each lily leaf, pipe a tube 3 curved line to lower center of adjacent ivy leaf. Complete outline of leaves and add dots. Outline and trim cross with same tube. For jewels, mix tinted piping gel with a little royal icing and pipe with tube 5.

4. Circle base of cake with green tube 20 upright shells. Just above them, fill in space up to marked line with tube 233 "fur." Fill in with tube 1. Roll a cylinder of marzipan to fit hole in cake. Ice top chocolate and cut a slit in center to receive cross. Set cylinder in hole and insert cross. Glaze jewels by brushing with corn syrup and present this royal tribute to Father. Cut ten slices from Turk's Head, six from base cake.

Candle-lit crowns
Quick & clever

Here's a bright way to tell Dad he's king of your heart. A very impressive treat that's simple to do.

1. Paint six plastic Cake Shelves with yellow thinned royal icing. Dry. Bake, fill and ice a two-layer 12″ hexagon tier and a single-layer 6″ hexagon tier. (Most every dad loves chocolate.) Assemble on serving tray.

2. Mark corners of cake sides with a 2½″ heart cutter. Decorate base tier with tube 17. Outline heart shapes with curves, then pipe reverse shell bottom and top borders. Do lettering on upper tier with tube 2, shell borders with tube 15. Push shelves into each side of cake. Insert candles in Candle-lit Crown holders and place on shelves and upper tier. Serve to 23 guests.

Full of wisdom

The wise old owl on this cake is just as knowledgable as the young graduate! He's easily formed with the versatile oval pan.

1. Bake a 9" x 13" x 4" two-layer sheet cake, and a 2" high oval cake. Fill the sheet cake, ice and place on a foil-covered cake board. Use *Celebrate! V* pattern to cut a cardboard cake base for the oval cake and place cake on it. Ice cake thinly with buttercream and build out ears with icing, shaping with spatula.

2. Transfer pattern to oval cake. Pipe tube 14 stars on head and ears. Outline eyes with tube 2, then flow in centers of eyes with thinned icing. Outline beak with tube 2 and flow in thinned icing. Ruffled breast feathers are piped with tube 104 and wings with tube 401. Add tube 18 zigzag around eyes.

3. On sheet cake, pipe tube 18 base shell border, tube 17 top shell border. Pipe tube 2 message on cake sides. Place owl on sheet cake. Roll up a 1½" strip of paper for center of diploma, tape and attach to base of owl with icing. Roll 2" side pieces with flaring ends and tape to center roll. Pipe tube 8 claws over the diploma. Brush eyes, beak and claws with corn syrup for shine. Serves 30.

Golden years ahead

Thrill the graduate with this breathtakingly beautiful cake trimmed with golden roses. It sends wishes of good luck and happiness.

1. Make Golden Jubilee Roses in advance with royal icing and tubes 104, 124 and 125 following the instructions on page 153. Pipe royal icing spikes on a few flowers. Pipe tube 67 leaves on wires and dry, then bind into clusters of three with floral tape.

2. Bake a 12" x 18" x 4" two-layer sheet cake and a single-layer horseshoe cake. Fill and ice the sheet cake, then place on a foil-covered cake board. Place horseshoe cake on a cake base cut the same size and shape as the cake, then ice. Mark position of horseshoe on sheet cake and insert dowel rods for support. Place horseshoe on sheet cake.

3. Pipe tube 17 base and top shell borders around horseshoe and down the corners. On sheet cake, pipe message on side with tube 16. Pipe tube 22 base shell border and tube 18 top border. Arrange roses and leaves on top of cake and at corners with mounds of icing. Serves 60.

50 happy years of decorating

You did it!

Graduation! Years of study end in a formal ceremony of achievement. Bring the graduates together for an evening of friendship, to talk of old times and the bright years ahead.

A new flower to make with your Flower Garden Cutters

Make sunny California poppies with your Flower Garden Cutters. These are the flowers that glorify the very special Mother's day cake on page 89.

The Flower Garden Cutter Set is very versatile! It needs only your imagination to create many new and different flowers beyond the 15 described in the instruction booklet that accompanies the cutters. The pink lilies on page 56 are another example of a new flower you can make with the cutters. Be creative — you'll think of many others.

When the flowers are finished, mount some on wire stems and pipe royal icing spikes on backs of others to trim cake. (See page 157.)

Make full-size poppies

For each flower, cut four petals from thinly rolled gum paste with the Small Violet Leaf Cutter. Working with one petal at a time, roll rounded edge on a piece of foam toweling with a modeling stick. Insert number 8 flower nail into a block of styrofoam. Lay petal on nail, point toward center, then roll three other petals and lay them on the nail. Cut a disc of thin gum paste with tube 2A. Brush the back of it with egg white and press it in the center of the flower. Dry. Make some full-size poppies following the same method, but shaping them in medium-size lily nails and using a disc cut with tube 11, for flowers that have not fully opened. Pipe centers with tubes 233 and 1. Dry. Brush centers of poppies with yellow powdered pastels and a small artist's brush. (To create powder, shave pastel sticks with a sharp knife.)

Make smaller poppies

Use the Briar Rose cutter for smaller flowers. Be sure gum paste has been rolled very thin before cutting the flower. Trim off one petal with a sharp knife. Make a cut, 1/8" long, between the remaining petals. Roll edges of each petal on a piece of foam toweling with a modeling stick. Cut a disc with tube 11, brush the back of it with egg white and place it in the center of the poppy. Place the flower on a sponge and press in the center with the round end of a modeling stick to form a cup shape. Dry, then pipe tube 1 centers.

Tiny poppies go quickly

Cut flowers from thin gum paste with the Violet Cutter and trim off one petal with a sharp knife. Roll the edge of each petal on a piece of foam toweling with a small modeling stick. Place poppy on a sponge and press in center with a modeling stick to form a cup shape. Dry, then pipe tube 1 centers.

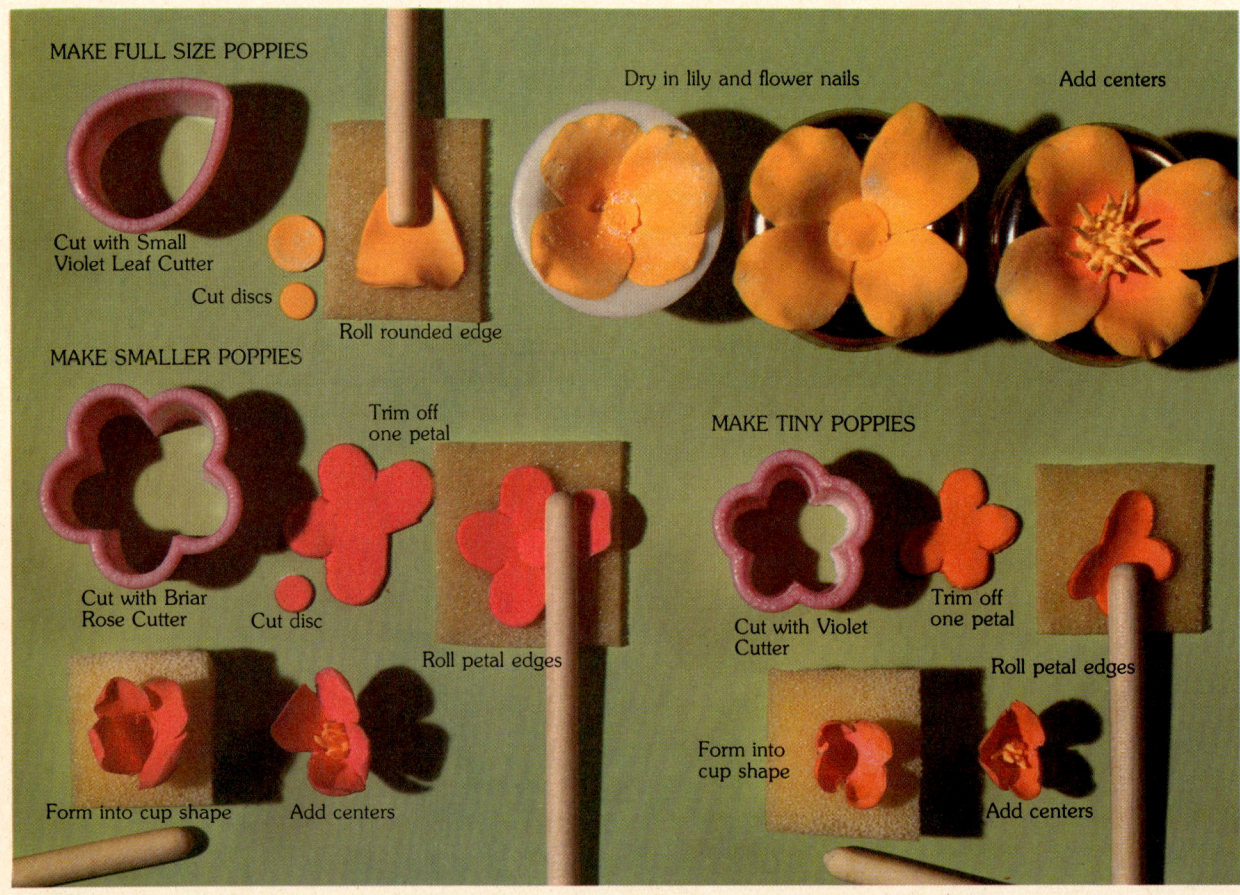

94

Celebrate!
THE SUNNY DAYS OF JULY AND AUGUST

An airy gazebo crowns a summer cake. Directions, page 108.

You'd be surprised how often we receive letters that ask "Can you give us ideas for simple cakes that look impressive and are easy to serve?" Here's a trio of happy answers that will inspire you to decorate lots of other fast, easy cake triumphs.

Just bake a sheet cake in a disposable shiny foil pan. Let it chill while you get out your cookie cutters and dream up a lavish design for the top. Almost any cutter will do—we used round and heart shaped—but think of the possibilities of stars, diamonds, boat shapes, even people and animals! If these are your first cakes patterned with cutters, you might want to get out a sheet of paper cut to the size of the cake top and experiment before you do the design in icing. A ruler and a pencil are the only tools you need.

Swirl on icing, imprint with the cutters, using them as pattern presses, then pipe the design with prettily tinted icing. Presto! A cake you'll be proud of.

Where do these beauties make their colorful appearance? In the summer, of course, at picnics! Also at barbecues, pool parties and porch get-togethers. In fall and winter they travel to school, club meetings, bake sales (no pan to return!) and tail-gate football feasts. They're perfect for graduation parties and class outings in the spring. Just any happy occasion where you need an easy-to-carry, fast-to-do dessert calls for one or more of these creative cakes.

Cupcakes, of course, are naturals for portable treats. We piped a quick flower pattern on ours and set them in a foil tray for a festive presentation.

One bit of advice for picnickers—boiled icing is the best choice for frosting and decorating. It withstands the heat and high humidity of summer much better than buttercream.

Cupcake flowers
Quick & clever

So bright and cheery, everyone will love these happy cupcake flowers!

Bake cupcakes using your favorite cake recipe or mix. When cool, swirl with boiled icing. See page 159 for recipe. Pipe the flowers with tube 22, making six shells in a circle and adding a rosette. Set the cupcakes in a foil tray and they're ready to go when you are!

Circle of stars
Quick & clever

A curving design covers the top of this cake—easy to decorate, easy to carry, easy to serve. Bake it in a foil roasting pan or other disposable foil pan. We used one about 11½" x 9" x 2¼". You can bake the cake in any size pan and adjust the pattern to suit.

Bake the cake using your favorite recipe or cake mix and cool completely. Leave it in the pan and ice the top with boiled icing. Measure the cake and press a 4" round cutter exactly in the center. Now line up a triple row of circles with a 1¾" cutter, intersecting where they cross the center circle. Outline circles with tube 15 stars. Within each small circle pipe a four-petaled shell flower with tube 15 and add a star in the center. Add more flowers between circles at ends of cake. Finish with a tube 17 star border.

Sweetheart fantasy
Quick & clever

A stunning design with an oriental look achieved by using warm, subtle colors. Bake the cake in a foil pan—ours is 11½" x 9" x 2¼".

Bake the cake using your favorite recipe or cake mix and cool completely in the pan. Ice the top of the cake with boiled icing. A 2" heart cutter makes the design. Find the exact center of the cake and mark. Imprint four hearts, points touching center mark. Add eight more hearts surrounding the first quartet, and finally one on both ends. Pipe the hearts with tube 16, then add fleurs-de-lis and shells with the same tube. Pipe tube 17 shell border.

1947. *"The classes started to build up, so we had to find a larger facility. I found an old lodge hall at 59th and Halsted on the third floor. I got all of our neighbors who were young and just out of the service, as I was, and we whitewashed the whole place. We had more stuff on the floor than we did on the walls and ceiling."* —NORMAN WILTON

Take it on a picnic!

Sunny skies, parades, picnics, patriotic cakes add up to

a glorious fourth!

Red and blue butterflies...
flutter over a field of white daisies.
1. Make Color Flow butterflies using *Celebrate! V* patterns. Outline with tube 1 and flow in thinned icing. Dry thoroughly. Pipe tube 1 designs on wings and dry. Pipe tube 3 body over the end of a length of fine wire and insert wings into wet icing, propping in position with cotton. Insert artificial stamens for antennae. Dry.
2. Pipe daisies with tubes 102 and 103. Add tube 5 centers. Dry within a curve.
3. Bake 10" x 4" two-layer and 6" x 2" single-layer, round tiers. Fill, ice and assemble on serving tray. On lower tier, pipe tube 16 base shell border. Divide side of tier into fourteenths. Drop a tube 16 string from point to point and add rosettes. Pipe tube 14 top shell border. Add tube 2 message.
4. On top tier, pipe tube 14 base shell border. Divide side into twelfths and pipe a tube 14 string from point to point on top of the lower tier. Trim with rosettes. Add tube 13 top shell border.
5. Secure daisies to cake. Trim with tube 65 leaves. Insert wires on butterflies into cake. Serves 17.

Calico star, Quick & clever
Trim a star-shaped cake with red, white and blue to celebrate the Fourth!
1. Pipe royal icing drop flowers with tube 225 and add tube 2 centers. Dry.
2. Bake a two-layer star cake. Fill, ice lightly and place on serving tray. Divide top of cake into five sections. Outline areas with tube 2. Cover entire cake with tube 16 stars. Secure drop flowers to cake in neat rows with dots of icing, trim with tube 65 leaves. Serves ten.

Blast off!
Trim a centerpiece cake with rockets to end the picnic with a bang!
1. Make rockets first. Bake three cakes in 6-ounce juice cans using a firm pound cake batter. Cut cardboard bases the same size as the cakes. Sharpen one end of three 8½" long dowel rods. Push each through a base, then through a cake so 1½" extends from top. Push cardboard up to cake, then wrap dowel right below it with masking tape to prevent slipping. Paint dowels with thinned royal icing. Dry. Insert dowels into a styrofoam block. Measure down from top of rocket 1¾" and pipe a line. Fill area above line with tube 13 stars, below line with tube 48 stripes. For tops, cut 5" circles and cut out one-third in a wedge. Roll remainder into a cone and glue. Pipe two heavy lines of icing around top of cakes and place paper cones in position.
2. Secure a half-ball of styrofoam in Heart Bowl with royal icing. Dry, then ice top with royal icing. Insert dowels into styrofoam in bowl, then push in three tapers behind them.
3. Bake a cake in the Ring-Shaped Mold and ice lightly. Cover with Quick Poured Fondant (see page 159). Place on serving tray after fondant has set, then pipe tube 22 bottom rosette border. Secure bowl in center hole. A spirited cake that serves 20.

A treasure box

Create this artful little box from gum paste, then fill it with one of the homemade candies on page 126.

1. Make a recipe of gum paste (see page 13). Roll out very thin and cut flowers with forget-me-not cutter. Curl petals by pressing from petal edge to center with a small modeling stick. Dry, then add tube 2 centers.

2. For box, roll out gum paste into an 11" circle, 3/16" thick. Mold the gum paste over a 6" hexagon pan that has been well-dusted with cornstarch. Trim the edge evenly with a sharp knife. Dry thoroughly, then remove from pan. Sand the edges and any rough places

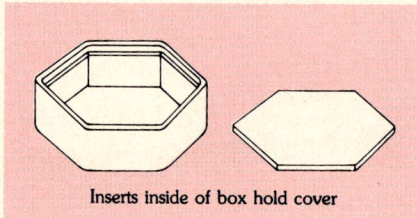
Inserts inside of box hold cover

on the outside.

3. Measure the inside of a side wall panel. Subtract 3/16" from the height and cut a cardboard pattern. Roll gum paste 1/8" thick and cut an insert, brush the back of it with egg white and press to inside of one wall panel. Continue cutting and attaching five more inserts (see diagram). Dry.

4. Turn box upside down, trace and cut a light cardboard pattern for cover. Trim pattern so it will rest on inserts inside of box. Roll gum paste 3/16" thick and cut cover. Dry.

5. Trim the box with designs molded in Baroque Regalia molds. Brush all pieces with egg white to attach. Make two center shells, curve and attach to cover, back-to-back to form handle. Make six center flowers and attach in the corners of cover. Mold a pair of side plumes and trim with a sharp knife to create "C" shapes, then attach them to one side of the box. Repeat for each of the remaining sides. Dry thoroughly. Secure forget-me-nots to box with dots

"Thank you" gifts

A box of candy, a basket of flowers, a bottle of wine—
these gifts say "Thank you" to your hostess in the nicest, newest way.

of royal icing, then dry. Spray with several coats of clear acrylic spray glaze to seal out moisture and protect the beauty of this little treasure for years.

A basket of flowers

A very pretty way to say "thank you for a lovely party".

1. Pipe many drop flowers using tubes 131, 191, 224 and 225. Add tube 2 centers and dry thoroughly.

2. Bake an 8" x 4" round, two-layer cake. Fill, ice and place on serving tray. Pipe basket weave on side with tube 48, then pipe tube 17 base rope border and tube 15 top rope border. Mound up icing a little on top of cake and secure drop flowers on dots of icing. Trim with tube 67 leaves. Serves ten.

A bottle of wine
Quick & clever

Easy to make, pretty to see and a joy for your hostess to receive!

1. Pipe a few drop flowers in advance with tube 190. Add tube 2 centers. Dry.

2. Bake a 14" x 2" square and a cake baked in half of the Bowling Pin pan. Cut square cake in half, fill and stack to make a 14" x 7" x 4" cake. Swirl on icing and place on a foil-covered cake board. Ice bowling pin cake lightly with buttercream and secure to cardboard cake base cut the same size and shape as the cake. Place on rack with pan beneath. Cover with Quick Poured Fondant (page 159). Let fondant harden, then place on rectangular cake.

3. On 14" x 7" cake, pipe tube 17 base shell border. Transfer *Celebrate! V* label pattern to bottle (or make your own). Outline with tube 2, then flow in thinned icing. Let harden, then pipe message and trim with tube 2, using tinted piping gel mixed with an equal amount of royal icing. Pipe the bottle cap with a tube 16 zigzag. Tie with a tube 1D ribbon, then add bow with tube 126. Trim with drop flowers. The wine bottle serves six, the rectangular cake serves 20.

101

Animal treasures—happy little cakes just for summer enjoyment

Why are children so charmed by animals? We don't know, but we're sure everyone will love these carefree animal cakes. Make a party, serve them on a sunny summer day with iced drinks.

Mischievous mice

Two plump fellows sit down to dinner, nicely served on a flowered plate.

1. Bake two half-eggs in Egg Minicake pan for bodies and ice. For heads, trim a marshmallow into a cone with scissors and insert a toothpick. For ears, roll one-third of a marshmallow flat and shape with fingers. Dip heads and ears into thinned buttercream icing and dry.

2. Stiffen buttercream with confectioners' sugar to a dough-like consistency. Form a ½" cube and cut diagonally into two wedges for cheese. Mark holes with a modeling stick. For plate, roll icing very thin on a cornstarch-dusted surface. Cut with a 2" round cutter, place on sponge and indent with number 2 flower nail. Dry, then paint design with food color.

3. Bake a 10" x 4" round, two-layer cake. Fill, ice and place on serving tray. Pipe tube 20 rosette base border. Divide side of cake into twelfths and drop a tube 16 string from point to point. Add rosettes. Trim strings with tube 224 drop flowers and tube 65 leaves. Pipe tube 17 top shell border.

4. Place half-eggs on cake top and cover with tube 13 stars. Build up stars for legs. Push toothpick on head into body and attach ears. Pipe tube 3 piping gel eyes and nose. Add tube 1 whiskers and tube 3 tail. Place plate of cheese in front. Serves 14.

Playful marzipan penguins

1. Roll a piece of brown marzipan (page 159) into a 3" long, 1" diameter cylinder for each penguin. Roll one end to shape head and beak. Press in tummy with back of a teaspoon dusted with cornstarch. Pinch bottom for feet and tail. Fill in tummy indentation with a 1¼" ball of untinted marzipan, attaching with egg white and smoothing with fingers. Cut claws on feet with small scissors. Insert a toothpick into penguin from bottom and stand upright. Bend head for quizzical expression. With small scissors, cut wings and bend outwards. Pipe royal icing eyes and dot center with brown food color. Dry, then brush with syrup glaze.

2. Bake an 8" x 4" round, two-layer cake. Fill, ice and place on serving tray. Mark a 4½" circle on cake top. Divide top and side of cake into twelfths and mark. Pipe a tube 2 outline around cir-

cle, then flow in thinned buttercream. Pipe tube 3 beading around top of cake, tube 5 around base. Pipe a triple row of tube 104 scallops on top of cake. Edge innermost row and center circle with tube 3 beading. Pipe tube 104 swags above base border, then four rows of tube 3 strings above them. Trim intersections with tube 3 curls of icing. A playful cake that serves ten.

Elephant amble

Star method and figure piping create the cutest cube cake of the season!

1. Pipe many tube 225 drop flowers with tube 2 centers. Pipe four tube 190 drop flowers with tube 2 centers. Dry, then mount on wire stems. Pipe four tube 65 leaves on wires, dry, then bind to stemmed flowers with floral tape.
2. Pipe heads of riders in advance using stiffened buttercream. Pipe four tube 12 balls on wax paper and insert a toothpick in each. Place in freezer.
3. Bake three 6" x 2" square layers. Fill and stack for a 6" cube. Ice smoothly and secure cake to cake board.
4. Trace *Celebrate!* V elephant pattern onto each side of cake with a toothpick. Outline with tube 2, then fill in with tube 16 stars. Pipe tube 2 vertical lines around bottom of cake then attach drop flowers with dots of icing.
5. Figure pipe the riders with stiffened buttercream. Pipe tube 12 body. Push toothpick on head into body. Pipe tube 7 arms and legs. Pipe eyes, nose, mouth and hair with tube 1. Make tube 32 star caps and add tube 2 balls. Insert stemmed flower in front of figure, then add tube 7 hands and feet. Slice into 12 generous servings.

If you'd like more servings, two elephants will fit on each side of a three-layer 12" square cake.

1948. *"It was just about this time we started teaching cake decorating to bakers under the GI Bill of Rights. We had 40 or 50 students per class—my dad, Mary Jane and Wesley, my brother and sister, and I taught the classes. My sister, Martha, wasn't with us then. She was living overseas with her husband, a colonel in the army."*
—NORMAN WILTON

Water pleasures

"I just purchased the gum paste figure molds—they're really delightful!" One of our readers wrote this note—you'll be just as delighted when you discover how easy and enjoyable it is to mold gum paste figures in the People Molds. Here the little figures give spirit and vivacity to two carefree summer cakes.

A call for help!
Serve this surfer cake after a day at the beach—everyone will laugh when you bring out this re-creation of a frequent event of the day.
1. Make a recipe of gum paste (page 13), tint a small portion and roll out ⅛" thick on a cornstarch-dusted surface. Cut out the surfboard with a sharp knife by tracing *Celebrate! V* pattern. Dry flat. Mold arms and upper figure in the man mold, following directions in the instruction booklet that comes with the mold. While pieces are still wet, cut off the torso at upper chest and left arm below shoulder as the picture shows. Dry thoroughly, then make up the face as booklet directs. Attach arms to torso.

Boil one tablespoon of water and one tablespoon of corn syrup for one minute. Use this glaze to quickly brush over man's figure and surfboard for a wet look. Pipe hair with royal icing, dry thoroughly and brush with glaze. Attach popsicle stick to back of surfboard with royal icing, with the end extending from the base.

2. Bake a two-layer 12" round cake. Fill and ice sides with buttercream. Stir a little white icing into blue boiled icing, leaving streaks of color unmixed. Ice top thickly, set man in position, and insert stick on surfboard in cake. Pull up waves with a spatula.

3. Finish the cake with a tube 21 base shell border and tube 17 top border. Pipe a colonial scroll on side of cake

with tube 16 and over-pipe for feathered effect. Serve this dramatic centerpiece to 22.

Backyard splash

What a cute surprise for the children! They'll be thrilled with this reproduction of their favorite summer fun.

1. Mold arms and upper torsos of children only, using 5-year-old and 10-year-old molds from the People Mold set. The accompanying booklet tells how. Roll out gum paste thinly, cut two 4½" circles, and use them to cover a 1½" diameter styrofoam ball, iced first with royal icing. Use egg white as glue. Cut a ¼" x 5" strip of gum paste and wrap around ball to cover seam. Trim excess, and dry.

2. When boy's torso is completely dry, roll a long cylinder, about ¾" in diameter, and wrap around figure for life preserver. Trim excess length at back and smooth seam. Dry. Cut a 1¾" x 3" strip from thinly rolled gum paste and wrap around girl's figure, trimming seam at back. Trim neckline and armholes. Dry. Make up the children's faces and attach arms. When girl's arm attachment is thoroughly dry, secure ball in her hands with tiny pieces of wet gum paste brushed with egg white. Keep ball propped on a 1" high object until joint is dry. Glaze figures the same as the surfer (opposite page), then pipe hair with tube 13. Dry hair, then glaze.

3. Pipe tube 33 royal icing drop flowers and dry. Bake and fill a 10" two-layer round cake. Set on cake board and ice sides thinly with buttercream. Cover sides with tube 2B stripes and pipe tube 233 grass at base. Press in drop flowers. Swirl boiled icing on cake top and set figures in position. Edge top with a tube 7 ball border. A summer pleasure that serves 14.

Why wait for a party?

Make one! Just bring out a pretty cake and start the fun!

Summertime—sunny days and breezy evenings put everyone in a party mood. Call friends and neighbors and decorate a festive cake to set the theme.

Say hello to a neighbor
Quick & clever

After the movers have left, greet a new neighbor with this happy cake.
1. Bake a 9″ x 13″ x 4″ two-layer sheet cake, a 6″ x 1″ petal layer and a 6″ x 1″ round layer. Cut leaves from round layer with 3¼″ boat cutter. Ice petal layer and leaves thinly with buttercream, then cover with tube 17 lines, following the contours of the cake.
2. Fill and ice the sheet cake, then secure to a foil-covered board. Cover sides with tube 4B vertical stripes. Pipe tube 20 base shell border, tube 18 top shell border. Transfer petal layer to sheet cake with a spatula. Pipe tube 8B flower stem, then position leaves. Pipe message with tube 14. Sheet cake serves 24, the sunflower is a bonus!

Golden day, golden cake

A beautiful cake for a sunny day, trimmed with goldenrod. Serve it outside on the porch with iced tea.
1. Bake a 12″ x 4″ two-layer petal cake. Fill, ice and place on serving tray. Pipe tube 16 base shell border. Add tube 16 fleurs-de-lis and scrolls on sides. Pipe tube 15 top shell border.
2. Pipe tube 2 goldenrod stems on top of cake and add tube 65 leaves. Pipe goldenrod on cake as described on page 154. Serves 26.

Sweet summer clover

Make this sweet cake the grand finale of your backyard barbecue.
1. Make royal icing clover blossoms and leaves in advance following the directions on page 155. Make 14 blossoms on wire stems, 12 without stems, 16 leaves on wire stems and 16 without stems. Bind stemmed leaves and blossoms into a bouquet with floral tape.
2. Bake a 10″ x 4″ round, two-layer tier and a 6½″ x 3″ round, two-layer tier, using Mini-tier pan. Fill the tiers and ice. Place lower tier on serving tray and top tier on 7″ Mini-tier separator plate. Insert dowel rods for support in lower tier, then place top tier in position.
3. On lower tier, pipe tube 8 bottom ball border, tube 7 top ball border. Divide side of tier into fourths. At each division, mark a scallop 2¾″ wide. Divide the areas between the scallops into thirds and drop string guidelines for three smaller scallops. Pipe garlands with tube 5 and a circular motion. Over-pipe with a tube 5 string, then a tube 2 string. This border is an adaptation of the one shown on page 151. Pipe tube 2 stems on side of cake within large scallops. Then attach clover blossoms and leaves with dots of icing.
4. On top tier, pipe tube 7 bottom ball border and tube 6 top ball border. Divide side of tier into twelfths and drop string guidelines from point to point. Pipe garlands the same as lower tier. Push a Flower Spike into center of top tier. Place bottom of a Petite Heart Base upside down over spike. Insert clover bouquet. Serves about 20.

Say "so long" to travelers
Quick & clever

Send friends on their way with a pretty cake trimmed with flags of the countries they will visit and appropriate flowers—forget-me-nots!
1. Make drop flower forget-me-nots using tubes 190 and 224.
2. Bake an 8″ x 4″ square, two-layer cake. Fill, ice and place on serving tray. Pipe tube 18 comma-shaped shells for base border, tube 17 top shell border. Print tube 13 message on cake sides.
3. Mark a 6″ circle on cake top, then secure flowers in a wreath on dots of icing. Push International Flags into center of cake top, then trim base of flags with flowers. Cluster flowers at corner of cake and insert an American flag to remind them of their stay-at-home friends. Trim all flowers with tube 65 leaves. Serves twelve.

1949. *"Every other two weeks we would have a class in one of the major bakery supply houses. We went back and forth all over the country teaching cake decorating to the bakers. Some of the students, after going to our class two or three times, became very good decorators, and started teaching classes themselves."*—NORMAN WILTON

AN AIRY GAZEBO CAKE
Shown on page 95

A pretty little summer house crowns a latticed daisy-strewn cake. Create it for an important anniversary, a wedding or for the centerpiece of any formal summer party.

1. Make royal icing trims first. Pipe daisies with tubes 101, 102 and 103. Add tube 5 centers and flatten with a fingertip dipped in tinted granulated sugar. Dry within a curved surface. Pipe a few tube 225 drop flowers with tube 2 centers to trim cherub. Dry.

Cover *Celebrate! V* lattice pattern with wax paper. Pipe outline and lattice with tube 2 and egg white royal icing. Dry. Over-pipe curves with tube 13 and dry.

2. Make the pretty gazebo. Secure a 9" hexagon separator plate inside Circus Tent Top with royal icing and dry. Wrap six 7½" Corinthian pillars with narrow ribbon, taping ends inside pillars. Place pillars on a 9" hexagon separator plate. Set tent top on pillars. Make six little ribbon bows and attach to tops of pillars with icing.

Pipe tube 1 lines over the divisions on the tent top, then fill between the lines with tube 1 "sotas" (curves and dots of icing, all touching). Pipe tube 2 dots along bottom edge. Paint a 6" length of florists' wire with royal icing and dry. For flower on top of tent top, pipe petals with tube 104, center with tube 5. Insert painted wire through center of flower into hole at peak of tent top. Dry. Cut paper pennant and do lettering with tube 1. Glue to painted wire, then add ribbon streamers and a tube 2 ball at top of wire.

3. Bake 14" x 4" round and 12" x 3" hexagon, two-layer tiers. Fill, ice and assemble on an 18" foil-covered cake board, using dowel rods for support in the lower tier.

4. On the lower tier, divide the side into sixths using the corners of the upper tier as a guide. Pipe a 3" high tube 22 upright shell at each division. Divide spaces between them into fourths and mark. Pipe a 2" high upright shell in the center and a 2¾" high upright shell on either side. Drop tube 16 strings and add tube 20 rosettes. Pipe tube 18 shells to complete the base border. Pipe tube 16 top shell border.

5. On upper tier, pipe tube 16 base shell border and tube 13 top shell border. Pipe lines of icing next to base border, and set lattice pieces in position, one by one. Trim lower edges of lattice and seams with tube 13 lines and rosettes. Set gazebo on tier top and edge separator plate with tube 13. Trim standing cherub with drop flowers and small daisies, securing with dots of icing. Trim with tube 65 leaves. Set cherub within gazebo and secure with a little icing. Finish the cake by trimming with daisies and tube 66 leaves. A summery centerpiece that cuts into 142 wedding-size servings.

Lift off the gazebo before serving to save as a pretty ornament.

1952. *"At that time we started to work on our first book,* The Wilton Encyclopedia of Modern Cake Decorating. *Since I wasn't a very good writer, I decided we would do this pictorially and show all the steps of decorating in pictures. My idea was that you could take this book to any country, and people wouldn't even have to know English to understand what cake decorating was all about."*—NORMAN WILTON

School time! Bake something bright to send to class

Welcome back, teacher

Start the new school year with a greeting for the teacher. Everyone in the class will enjoy the treat!

1. Make gingerbread (recipe on page 19) or your favorite roll-out cookie dough (a good recipe is on page 8). Roll out the dough and cut out the children using the small cutter from the Gingerbread Cutter Set. Bake the cookies and cool, then decorate them with royal icing. Outline with tube 1, thin the icing and flow in areas. Let the icing set, then add tube 1 facial features, hair and trims on clothes. Use tube 101 to make ruffles. Dry thoroughly. Secure toothpicks to the backs of two cookies with royal icing so they extend from one leg. Attach a bamboo skewer or drink mixer to the back of a third cookie so it extends from the center of the bottom of the cookie. These are for the children jumping rope on the top of the cake.

2. Bake, fill and ice an 8″ x 4″ round, two-layer cake. Place on a foil-covered cake board. Pipe tube 7 bottom bulb border, tube 5 top bulb border. Add tube 2 lettering. Secure cookies to side of cake with icing, then drop a tube 2 string for jump rope for each. Push the skewer on the one cookie into the top of the cake so the child is suspended as if he was jumping. Push the toothpicks on the remaining two cookies into the top of the cake on either side of the jumping child. Pipe a tube 2 jump rope between them. Serves ten.

Apples for the students
Quick & clever

Here's an easy way to make cute treats to bring to school.

Bake cupcakes using your favorite cake

recipe or mix. Swirl on boiled icing or buttercream. Add a cherry candy to the top of each cupcake, then trim it with a tube 3 stem and tube 65 leaf. You've created little apple cakes!

Happy days!
Is your pre-schooler feeling a little left-out now that the older children are in school? Bake this sheet cake slate and let him preside at a party when the students come home from school. He'll feel so important!

1. Pipe the pieces of chalk in advance on wax paper. Use royal icing and tube 2A, making them 3¼" long. Dry.

2. Bake a 9" x 13" single-layer sheet cake. Ice and secure to a foil-covered cake board. Use a decorating comb to make ridges on the sides of the cake. Pipe slate frame around top of cake with tube 1D, holding the tube with the ridges up. Add tube 3 writing.

3. Pipe two tube 3 lines across the upper portion of the cake for the abacus. Add counting beads by piping balls with tube 10. Keep tip of tube buried in icing while piping for rounded shapes. Stop pressure and pull away. Lay the chalk on the edge of the cake. Serves twelve.

50 happy years of decorating

Bake a batch of cookie treats! They're perfect for the children to take to school. You can make ones for the first letters of the children's names, cookies to spell out a message, or even make the whole alphabet! The choice is yours. Patterns for the letters are in *Celebrate! V Pattern Book*. You design the cute trims, matching the design with the cookie letter. It's fun!

Bake the cookies

First, trace the letter patterns onto pieces of light cardboard and cut out. Make a recipe of Roll-Out Cookie dough (see page 8 or use your own favorite). Roll out the dough on a floured cookie sheet, then place it in the freezer until firm. Remove from freezer, place patterns on dough and cut around them with a sharp knife. Remove the excess dough from around the letters. Place the cookie sheet back in the freezer until the dough is very firm. You can bake more cookies on a sheet, the cookies hold their shape better and there is less spreading when the dough is frozen before baking. Bake at 375°F for about eight minutes. Remove from cookie sheet and allow to cool.

Decorate the letters

Decide which designs you are going to use for the letters. Take a look at the list at right for some ideas. Make a few sketches, if you wish, to determine how the designs will be positioned on the letters. Be creative!

Next, decide what your palette of colors will be for decorating the designs. Try to stay with four or five colors to keep it simpler and for better effect. Make a recipe of buttercream icing (see page 159) and tint small portions in the colors you have chosen.

Most of the designs we chose to use were piped using tubes 1 and 2. Tube 6 was used for larger ball shapes and tube 101 was used to pipe the rose. Some of the shapes were figure piped and others were outlined with tube 2, the icing thinned a little and then flowed in. All cookies were outlined with tube 2.

Some idea starters

Here are some ideas for designs for each letter of the alphabet. These are just a few—the possibilities are endless. Look in the dictionary for more ideas.

A—anchor, apple, acorn, airplane
B—boat, ball, bell, banana, block, bee
C—corn, candle, cherries, carrot
D—duck, dog, dinosaur, dolphin
E—envelope, egg, eight ball, eye, ear
F—flag, fan, feather, fern, fish
G—grapes, ghost, globe, guitar, gun
H—heart, hand, hat, hammer, haystack, helmet
I—indian, ice cream, igloo, iron
J—jack-in-the-box, jar, jellybeans
K—kite, key, king, knot, knight
L—light bulb, ladder, lamb, lamp
M—moon, mitten, magnet, mushroom, mop, monkey
N—note, nail, needle, nest, net
O—oil can, onion, oak leaf, ornament
P—peas, peanut, pencil, paddle, palm
Q—queen, question mark, quilt
R—rose, rocket, ring, rabbit, raft, rake
S—shamrock, sun, snake, saw, shovel
T—teepee, turtle, tree, table, thimble
U—umbrella, unicorn
V—violet, vacuum cleaner, vest, vine
W—worm, watermelon, wheel, wishing well, whale, whip
X—xylophone
Y—yarn, yardstick
Z—zipper, zebra

1963. *"The business kept building up, so we built a second building at 115th Street and Halsted. It had 25,000 square feet and we added on to it about every two years. We built it up to 180,000 square feet, with about 400 working there."*—NORMAN WILTON

Halloween horrors

Celebrate Halloween with Quick & clever cakes. They're fun to make!

Perk up the costume party with these spooky, quick-to-make cakes. Each is just right for a scary Halloween party—everyone will love them!

Glowing Jack-o'-lanterns
Top a sheet cake with cookie jack-o'-lanterns. The eyes, noses and mouths are made of hard candy, baked with the cookies to give an eerie glow.

1. Use the cookie recipe on page 8. Tint a portion orange and a smaller portion green by kneading in liquid food color. Keep remainder of dough tightly wrapped in plastic. Line a cookie sheet with foil, shiny side up, and coat well with cooking oil. Roll out dough and cut around *Celebrate! V* patterns (or make your own) with a sharp knife. Use holly cutters from the Flower Garden Set for leaves. Lay jack-o'-lanterns on prepared cookie sheet and lay leaves in place. Crush two sour ball candies for each jack-o'-lantern and place the candy pieces in the openings for the eyes, nose and mouth. Bake at 375° F for about eight minutes. Candy will have melted into transparent color! Cool until candy hardens, then peel off foil. You may wish to bake more to give to the party guests.

2. Bake a 9" x 13" x 2" single-layer sheet cake. Ice and place on a foil-covered cake board. Pipe tube 18 comma-shaped base shell border. Pipe tube 18 top shell border.

3. Attach two popsicle sticks to the back of each jack-o'-lantern with royal icing so about half of the sticks extend from the bottom of the cookie. Dry, then insert sticks into top of cake. Pipe tube 3 grass around cookies, concealing sticks. Serve to twelve party guests. For dramatic presentation, place squat candles behind the cake, light them and darken the room!

Man in the moon
On Halloween, if it's a clear night, you're sure to see the man in the moon looking down on the festivities. Bring him right in to the party on this quick-to-make cake.

1. Bake, fill and ice a 10" x 4" round, two-layer cake. Place on foil-covered cake board. Pipe rosette borders using tube 17 on bottom, tube 16 on top.

2. Transfer *Celebrate! V* pattern to cake top. Outline moon with tube 3, stars with tube 2. Fill outlined areas with tube 14 stars. Pipe eye with tube 5. Add message with tube 3. Serves 14.

Boo in the night
What could be more appropriate on this night of spooks than a scary ghost? This one is just trying to be friendly, so let him join the party!

1. Bake cake in the Bowling Pin pan. Chill, fill the two halves, securing with toothpicks and cut 1½" from bottom of cake. Secure to foil-covered cake board. Push three regular size marshmallows onto a long bamboo skewer for each arm. Insert the ends of the skewers into the cake. Ice with boiled icing, spreading it thickly to create a ghostly figure. Pipe tube 7 bulbs around base of ghost. Push plastic Black Bats into icing on head and one arm, then pipe eyes and mouth with tinted piping gel and tube 6.

2. Garnish the cake board with plump pumpkins. Pipe them around regular size marshmallows. Push a fork into the marshmallow, then pipe around the middle with tube 10 to make fatter and rounder. Begin piping at bottom of marshmallow and pull tube 10 lines of icing up to top all around. Let icing stiffen, then remove pumpkins from forks and secure to board beside ghost. Trim with tube 67 leaves and tube 3 vines. (These make good trims for sheet cakes, too.) Serve to twelve.

Pumpkin patch
Each of these cute, perfect pumpkin cakes is shaped using two Blossom cakes. They're easy to make.

1. For each pumpkin, bake two cakes in the Blossom Pans. Chill, then slice off small end of one cake for base. Ice wider side and set second cake on it. Attach to a cardboard cake base the same size with icing.

2. Cover with tube 16 stars, then pipe stem with tube 6B, turning hand as you pipe for a twisted effect. Trim with tube 67 leaves. Each pumpkin serves two.

Yes, there are flowers, lovely ones, to pipe right on a cake.
Have fun with tubes and experiment with ones new to you.
As you look over your tubes, you'll discover many more ways to pipe quick flowers.

Cherry blossom

These flowers are formed in two very easy steps. With tube 1F held at a 90° angle to the decorating surface, squeeze the decorating bag, stop pressure and pull away. It's really a drop flower. Add center with just one squeeze of the bag fitted with tube 233. These blossoms are so easy and give such a beautiful effect. Practice them first, then trim a springtime cake!

Decorate the cake. Bake a 10" x 4" two-layer, round cake. Fill and ice, then place on serving tray. Pipe tube 17 base shell border. Divide side of cake into twelfths and mark. Drop double tube 13 strings between the marks. Top the intersections of the strings with hearts piped with tube 13. Pipe tube 15 top shell border. Using divisions on side of cake as a guide, divide top of cake into sixths. Pipe a cluster of cherry blossoms at each division. Trim with slender tube 65 leaves. Serves 14.

Bearded iris

This lovely summer flower is easily piped right on the cake. Pipe the top of the flower first. Using tube 32, pipe curved shell on left, then another on the right, overlapping at the top. For lower part of flower, pipe two outer curved shells, then center shell. Add "beards" with tube 2 on the lower part of the flower. Practice first, then you'll be ready to pipe them right on the cake.

Decorate the cake. Bake, fill and ice a 9" x 13" x 4" two-layer sheet cake. Place on a foil-covered cake board. Pipe tube 17 rosettes around base of cake and tube 16 fleurs-de-lis above them. Make a mark in the icing on top of the cake at each place you wish to position an iris. Pipe a tube 15 stem to each mark and add leaves with the same tube, making two or three strokes of the tube for each leaf. Pipe irises at the marks as described above, then add tube 15 top shell border. Serves 24.

Shaggy chrysanthemum

These quick fall flowers add a special sparkle to a happy cake. They are easy to pipe and trim a cake in a hurry. For each flower, pipe a round mound of icing as a base with tube 199. Beginning at top of mound, pull out many strands of icing with tube 233 until it is completely covered.

Decorate the cake. Bake, fill and ice a 9" x 13" x 3" two-layer sheet cake. Place on a foil-covered cake board. Pipe tube 8 bottom bulb border and tube 5 top bulb border. Mark a slightly elongated circle in the icing on top of the cake with a toothpick as guide in piping flowers. Write tube 2 message. Pipe the flowers, one at a time, along the marked circle as described above. Position them so they just touch the ones on either side of them. Pipe the flowers at the corners of the cake right in position. Trim with tube 67 leaves. Serves 24.

116

Autumn! There's a tang in the air that makes one eager to plan new projects, prepare for parties and brush up on skills. Here are two stunning centerpieces for fall gatherings—they'll inspire you to create your own.

A cake for your sweetheart
Quick & clever

We decorated this charmer for Sweetest Day, but it could grace any occasion. The spiral treatment on top is so easy and effective you'll want to adapt it for other cakes.

1. Bake an 8″ two-layer round cake. Fill and ice smoothly with buttercream. Place on a rack with a pan beneath it and cover with Quick Poured Fondant (page 159). This is the quickest way we know to achieve a smooth glossy coating—and it sets off piping beautifully. When fondant has set, place cake on serving tray.

2. Pipe tube 6 base ball border, then drop triple tube 2 strings on side of cake, keeping them ¼″ apart. Trim with dots and hearts. Pipe name on top with same tube. Now, starting about 1″ in from edge, pipe a spiral line. Don't worry if the line breaks—flowers will cover it. Pipe tube 104 rosebuds right on the cake and finish the cake with tube 66 leaves.

For variations, change the color scheme, and substitute sweetpeas or drop flowers for the rosebuds. This is a spur-of-the-minute cake you'll be proud of! Serves ten.

A splendid Thanksgiving

This golden cake really celebrates autumn! The brilliant trim is made of marzipan. If you haven't used this versatile material before, here is a good project to begin with. Marzipan takes color readily, tastes delicious and gives a rich Continental look to a cake. And it's so easy to use—if you've ever played with modeling clay, or rolled out a pie crust, you can trim this cake.

1. Make a recipe of marzipan and tint (page 159). For leaves, roll it out on a cornstarch-dusted surface or wax paper. Cut maple leaves with cutter from Flower Garden set. Dry within a curved surface, then brush with glaze.

Model fruit and vegetables. Pumpkin is 2″ across, scored with a stick, apples are ¾″ balls, ears of corn are 2½″ long. Score the corn for kernels and add slender husks. Grapes are small balls of marzipan attached with egg white. Dry all pieces, then brush with glaze.

2. Bake a 14″ x 2″ single layer and a 10″ x 4″ two-layer round tier. Ice the 14″ tier, place on cake board and insert a ring of ¼″ dowel rods to support upper tier. Fill and ice the 10″ tier and center on lower tier. On the 14″ tier, pipe tube 32 base shell border and tube 18 top shell border. Pipe tube 19 base shell border on the 10″ tier. Pipe triple tube 32 shells around the top of the tier and add tube 19 fleurs-de-lis and stars beneath them. Make a wreath of maple leaves around the 10″ tier, securing with icing. Arrange the marzipan harvest on top. Serves 32.

1956. *"We moved into a small store on the corner of 67th and Wentworth and I made it a bridal cake shop. The street was very busy and the store was by a stop light, so as the cars came up, they would stop and look in the windows. We would keep them lit all night."*
—NORMAN WILTON

Autumn glories

On their 35th anniversary, surprise them with a party and a lovely cake

Jade is the recommended gift for couples celebrating their 35th anniversary, so icing facsimiles of that lovely stone trim this handsome cake.

1. Do heart and oval "jade" stones in Color Flow. Outline with tube 2, flow in thinned icing, dry and edge with tube 1. Do oval plaque for top of tier by outlining with tube 5 and flowing in with icing the consistency of honey for a rounded look. Dry thoroughly.

2. Bake a 12" x 4" two-layer round tier and an oval single-layer tier. Fill the 12" tier, ice both tiers and assemble. Divide lower tier side into sixths. Transfer *Celebrate! V* patterns to both tiers.

3. On 12" tier, pipe bottom border with tube 18. Just below each marked side design pipe three upright shells and a star, then complete shell border. Pipe tube 18 reverse shell border on top. Pipe side designs, using tube 18 for center part, tube 16 for outer scrolls.

4. Pipe frame on oval tier. Secure oval plaque in center, then pipe radiating tube 16 lines around it. Border plaque with tube 16 shells. Pipe outer scrolls with tube 13. Do fancy numbers with tube 1. Pipe tube 16 top and bottom borders, then pipe side designs with same tube. Attach "jade" stones with dots of icing. This stunning cake serves party-size pieces to 28 guests.

Here is a traditional list of anniversary gifts that will suggest cake trims:

1st—paper
2nd—cotton
3rd—leather
4th—fruit, flowers
5th—wood
6th—iron
7th—copper
8th—bronze
9th—pottery
10th—aluminum
11th—steel
12th—silk
14th—ivory
15th—crystal
20th—china
25th—silver
30th—pearl
35th—jade
40th—ruby
45th—sapphire
50th—gold
55th—emerald
60th—diamond
75th—diamond

Copper is the appropriate gift for a seventh anniversary

Create this charming copper kettle, fill it with nasturtiums and set it on a calico-printed cake! The anniversary couple will never forget this celebration!

1. Make about 24 royal icing nasturtiums in advance. Line a 1⅝" lily nail with foil. Pipe five ruffled, separated petals with tube 103, then join in center with a tube 6 dot. Push in artificial stamens. When dry, mount the flowers on wire stems (page 157).

Pipe round leaves with tube 104 on a number 7 flower nail. Dry, then add tube 1 lines. Mount on wire stems just as you would a flower.

2. Now for the tea kettle! Bake a cake in one-half of the ball pan and a 6" x 2" round cake using a firm pound cake recipe. Fill the two cakes, placing half-ball on top, and secure to a 6" cake circle. Cover with rolled fondant, following the instructions on page 29. Roll two long, thin strings of fondant and attach one around bottom, one around top of kettle with egg white. Mark a groove with the back of a knife around side about 3" up from base. Push a Flower Spike into the top of the tea kettle. Hand-model a fondant spout about 3" long, insert a thin dowel, brush base with egg white and insert in side of kettle. Model a 2½" handle, then attach to kettle with egg white. Join handle to top of kettle with thin strings of fondant.

3. Bake, fill and ice a 10" x 3" round, two-layer cake. Mark center with a 6" cake circle and insert dowels, clipped level with top, within it. "Print" rest of cake with tube 1 stylized flowers. Pipe tube 7 base bulb border, tube 5 top border. Place kettle on top of cake, then arrange flowers in the flower spike, and add a few blooms to the 10" cake. Letter a paper card with tube 1, attach a ribbon bow, and fasten to cake with icing. Kettle serves nine, the base cake serves 14.

A golden cake for our golden jubilee
Shown on front and back covers

Ablaze with 50 candles and adorned with 50 Golden Jubilee Roses, this spectacular cake marks Wilton's half century. Adapt it for the golden anniversary of someone you know, or change the color scheme for a magnificent wedding cake.

1. Make the flowers in advance—then trimming the cake with simple but lavish looking borders will go quickly. Make 50 Golden Jubilee Roses with tube 126 as described on page 153. Also make many smaller Jubilee Roses, sweet peas and rosebuds with tube 104. Dry, then mount three large Jubilee Roses on wire stems. Pipe royal icing spikes on the backs of the rest and on most of the smaller roses.

2. Spray five 7½" Corinthian pillars gold and dry. Glue five stud plates to the flat sides of each of two 14" separator plates from Crystal-Clear Cake Divider set. Dry, then paint with thinned royal icing and dry again.

3. Bake round tiers—18" x 6" is three layers high. 14" x 4", 10" x 4" and 6" x 3" tiers are two layers high. Assemble on a 22" round, foil-covered plywood or masonite board. Insert ½" dowel rods in the two lower tiers for support and ¼" dowels in the 10" tier, all clipped off level with tier tops.

4. Pipe tube 17 base shell border on 18" tier. Divide side of tier into fifths, using pillars as guide. At each division trace *Celebrate! V* scallop pattern, then pipe zigzag garlands on the pattern with tube 15. Pipe a pair of tube 18 zigzag garlands topped with a fleur-de-lis at base of cake between the scallop patterns. Add tube 20 reverse shell top border and tube 17 reverse shells around separator plate.

Pipe tube 16 base shell border around 14" tier. Divide side of tier into fifteenths and pipe tube 17 zigzag garland from point to point. Top every third intersection with a tube 18 fleur-de-lis. Add tube 19 reverse shell top border. On 10" tier, pipe tube 18 base shell border, tube 18 reverse shell top border. Divide tier into tenths and pipe a tube 18 fleur-de-lis at every other division.

On 6" top tier, pipe tube 17 borders—shells at base, reverse shells at top. Divide side of tier into fifths.

5. Attach the flowers to the tiers as pictured with royal icing. Secure a mound of smaller roses, rosebuds and sweet peas to the separator plate, then attach five Candle Holder Wreaths between the pillars with icing. Trim wreaths with small roses, rosebuds and sweet peas. Trim all the flowers with gold artificial leaves. Insert Push-In holders in the sides of the tiers for candles and trim with tube 15 rosettes. Use 20 holders in 18" tier, 15 in 14" tier, ten in 10" tier and five in 6" tier. The three lower tiers serve wedding-size servings to 288, the top tier serves 16.

50 GLORIOUS YEARS
Shown on page 109

Fluffy chrysanthemums garland a golden anniversary cake. With just a few changes, it's lovely for a fall wedding.

1. Make chrysanthemums in advance with royal icing. Pipe a tube 9 ball on a flower nail. Add petals with tube 81. Pipe small mums in yellow and white, large mums in yellow, rose and deep rose. Dry, then pipe a tube 5 royal icing spike on the backs of most of the flowers. Pipe lobed leaves with tube 104. Dry within a curved surface.

2. Glue Anniversary Years numerals to a Petite Decorator Base for ornament. Paint ornament, four 5" Corinthian pillars and two 8" separator plates with thinned royal icing and dry. Glue Anniversary Couple to Petite Heart Base.

3. Bake 14" x 4" and 10" x 4" square, two-layer tiers and a 6" x 3" round, two-layer tier. Fill, ice and assemble on an 18" cake board. Use dowel rods for support in two lower tiers.

4. On base tier, pipe tube 21 bottom rosette border. Pipe tube 18 shells down the corners and around top edge of tier. Mark scallops on side with a toothpick, then pipe with tube 16 and add rosettes. Pipe tube 3 names.

Pipe tube 18 shells around all edges of middle tier. Pipe "C"-shaped scrolls on side with tube 16. Add fleurs-de-lis in corners and hearts. Edge separator plate with tube 16.

Pipe tube 16 shell borders on top tier. Divide side into eighths. Pipe tube 16 "C"-shaped scrolls between the divisions, leaving a 1" space between them. Attach leaf and small mum in spaces. Secure anniversary couple to cake top and surround with white mums.

5. Attach numeral ornament between pillars with icing, then secure mums to cake as pictured. Trim all flowers with leaves, securing with icing. Two lower tiers provide 148 wedding-size servings, top tier serves 16.

Celebrate!
HOLIDAY FUN IN NOVEMBER AND DECEMBER

A Sugar Plum village.
Decorating directions, page 136

Time to plan for Christmas baking!
Here are traditional treats to delight the children—each with a fresh new trim.

124

Christmas dolls

Brightly dressed dolls sit on a sheet cake. Every little girl will love them!

1. Make dolls first. Bake six half-eggs in Egg Minicake pan. Chill, fill the halves and secure with toothpicks. Trim bases of eggs so they sit firmly. Secure to a cake base the same size as egg and ice. Place on a sheet of wax paper.

Dress doll in yellow first. Pipe legs with tube 1A, then add tube 102 ruffles for panties. Pipe head with tube 2A and neck ruffle with tube 101. Add ruffle to front of dress with tubes 44 and 101s. Pipe ruffle for skirt with tube 127, add tube 46 band. Add tube 2A puff sleeves and arms, tube 4 thumbs. Trim sleeve with tube 101 ruffle. Pipe tube 2A shoes with tube 2 laces. Add hair, bow and features with tube 2. Trim dress with tube 1 dots.

Dress pink and green dolls the same way, using your imagination to create a different dress for each.

2. Bake a 9" x 13" x 4" two-layer sheet cake. Fill, ice and place on cake board. Pipe tube 18 base shell border, tube 16 shells around top border and down corners. Divide long sides of cake into eighths, short sides into sixths. Drop tube 14 strings and trim with rosettes. Mark an 8" x 11" oval on cake top and pipe with tube 14 scallops. Remove dolls from wax paper and secure to cake. Cake serves 24, each doll serves one delighted little girl.

Rocking horses

Make these darling gingerbread horses as place markers for a holiday table. They really rock!

1. Make gingerbread (recipe on page 19) roll out ⅛" thick on wax paper. Chill. Cut around *Celebrate!* V pattern with a sharp knife, dusting knife often with flour. Remove excess dough, then invert onto cookie sheet and peel off paper. Bake and cool. Make one facing left, one right for each horse.

2. Decorate horses with royal icing. Outline blanket with tube 2 and flow in thinned icing. Dry. Pipe tube 2 trims. Add a tube 14 star, or print child's name. Dry. Assemble with icing, securing half of a miniature marshmallow between bodies at front legs and one at back legs. Fill top seam with icing. Dry, flow in blanket on top and add trim.

Cookies for the tree

Here's a new use for your candy molds —use Stars and Shapes and Christmas Figures molds to shape lovely traditional cookies with old world charm. They're beautiful to serve unadorned —but here we accented the details with bright icing to hang on the tree.

1. Make a recipe of gingerbread (page 19). Break off a small portion and roll ½" thick. Dust mold with flour using a pastry brush, then brush off excess. Press dough into mold and trim excess. Crack mold down onto surface and shape will fall out. Place on lightly greased cookie sheet.

2. Place sheet in freezer for ten minutes to help preserve details, then bake immediately in 350°F oven for about ten minutes. As soon as gingerbread is removed from oven, cut hole for hanging with tube 2. Cool as directed in recipe, then trim with tube 2 and royal icing. String gold cord through hole to hang.

50

A prize assortment of Christmas candies made from McKinley Wilton's original recipes

1912. *"My dad, Dewey McKinley Wilton, started working in a candy factory when he was 14 or 15 years old. By the time he was 19 he was a foreman. Various men in the factory were specialists in hard candy, chocolates, caramels or creams, but as a foreman, he was proficient in all kinds of candy. He was a great candy maker."* —NORMAN WILTON

Here is a little sampling of McKinley Wilton's great candies. Pastry chef Larry Olkiewicz followed his recipes exactly to produce an array of absolutely delicious sweets.

Schedule a candy-making party for your family before Christmas. Then wrap each piece in clear plastic, pack in pretty containers and give to best-loved friends as princely gifts.

Peanut Brittle

Crunchy, nutty, with an enticing salt-sweet flavor—everybody's favorite.

- 2 cups granulated sugar
- 1½ cups corn syrup
- 1 cup water
- 2 cups salted peanuts
- 1 teaspoon baking soda
- ½ teaspoon salt
- 1 teaspoon butter

Combine sugar, corn syrup and water. Boil without stirring until temperature reaches 300°F. Add butter and peanuts, reduce heat and stir for one minute over low heat. Remove from heat and add salt and baking soda. Mix well. Spread in a thin layer on a buttered cookie sheet. Cool, then break into pieces. Makes 2¼ pounds.

Salt Water Taffy

An old-fashioned favorite of youngsters. They love pulling—and eating it!

- 3 cups granulated sugar
- 2 cups corn syrup
- 1 cup water
- 1 tablespoon butter
- ½ teaspoon salt
- 1 teaspoon vanilla
- Liquid food coloring

Combine sugar, corn syrup, butter and water. Bring to a boil and stir until temperature reaches 260°F. Stir in salt, vanilla and food coloring. If you wish to tint batch more than one color, divide after adding salt and vanilla, then add food coloring. Grease a pan and dust it with flour, then pour candy onto pan to cool. Pull with greased hands about 75 times. The more you pull, the lighter the taffy. Roll on a flour-dusted table into cylinders about the thickness of your index finger. Cut into 1" pieces. Makes 2 pounds of taffy.

English Toffee

Just divine! It's hard to believe just four ingredients can combine into something so delicious.

- 1 pound butter
- 3 cups granulated sugar
- 1 cup roasted finely chopped almonds
- 1 pound dark sweet chocolate

Melt butter and add sugar, stirring constantly, until golden brown or 290°F. Spread on greased cookie sheet and cool in refrigerator.

Shave and melt the chocolate in a double boiler and cool to about 93°F. Spread half of the chocolate on the top with a spatula. Sprinkle with half of the almonds. Place in refrigerator. When set, turn over onto wax paper and remove pan. Spread remaining chocolate on toffee and sprinkle with the remaining almonds. When chocolate has hardened, break into pieces. Makes 2¾ pounds of English Toffee.

French Nougat

A luxurious treat, not too sweet. The fine-textured nougat is enriched by a dark chocolate coating.

- 3 cups granulated sugar
- 2 cups corn syrup
- 1½ cups water
- 1 teaspoon vanilla
- 1 teaspoon butter
- 3 egg whites
- 1 teaspoon almond flavor
- 1½ cups roasted filberts, chopped
- 1 level teaspoon salt
- 1 pound dark sweet chocolate

Combine sugar, corn syrup, water and boil to 275°F. Add slowly to well-beaten egg whites. Beat until heavy. Add salt, flavoring and butter, then fold in the chopped nuts. Spread ¾" thick on a buttered cookie sheet, dusted with flour. Cut in small pieces.

To dip in chocolate, temper the chocolate as described on page 33. Reheat just until chocolate is barely liquid. Lay a piece of nougat on top of the chocolate and push down with the left index finger until chocolate just comes up over the edge. Lift out with a bent fork held in the right hand and place on wax paper. Yields 2¾ pounds.

Divinity Kisses

Light and airy with the surprise crunch of nuts and tropic sweetness of dates.

- ½ cup water
- 2 cups granulated sugar
- 2 tablespoons light corn syrup
- Pinch cream of tartar
- 1 cup chopped walnuts
- 1 cup chopped dates
- 2 egg whites
- 1 teaspoon vanilla
- Pinch salt

Combine sugar, corn syrup, water and cream of tartar. Cook without stirring and wash down crystals from side of pan occasionally with a pastry brush dipped in water. Cook to 248°F (soft ball test). Meanwhile, beat egg whites to a peak. Slowly add syrup to egg whites and beat with a mixer for at least 20 minutes until heavy. Add vanilla and salt. Fold in nuts and dates. Let set for one hour. Drop on wax paper with a teaspoon. Yields 1½ pounds.

New Orleans Pralines

You'll want to keep a tray of these near the tree for take-home gifts for visitors. The finest pralines you've ever tasted!

- 2 cups granulated sugar
- 1 cup brown sugar
- 1½ cups pecan pieces
- 1½ cups water
- 1 or 2 drops copper food color
- Pinch cream of tartar

Combine all ingredients and bring to a boil. Wash down sides of the pan with a pastry brush dipped in water. Boil to 236°F, remove from heat and stir for four or five minutes. Spoon out on wax paper to form patties about 3½" in diameter. Makes about eight patties.

Bring the magic and sparkle of Christmas to your home. The star is the symbol of the season so use it to shape these bright creations. They'll charm the children—grown-ups too.

Dazzle a dessert
Quick & clever

The simplest gelatin dessert takes on a festive air when it's trimmed with glittering stars!

GELATIN STAR TRIMS
- 2 three-ounce packages flavored gelatin
- 1 cup water

Bring water to a boil in a pan, remove from heat, add gelatin and stir until dissolved. Re-heat, if necessary, to completely dissolve the gelatin, but do not boil. Pour to a depth of ½" into a pan coated with cooking oil. Refrigerate until firm. Unmold onto a sheet of wax paper. Brush the inside of a star cookie cutter with cooking oil, then cut stars. This fruit flavored candy can be stored in the refrigerator, well-covered, for a week or longer.

Make lemon gelatin according to package directions and pour into a square or rectangular pan to a depth of 1". Chill overnight, then remove from pan. Cut into 4" squares, place each on a plate and add a gelatin star trim on top. Serve with a rosette of whipped cream.

Spangle a wreath
Quick & clever

Bright star cookies trim the showiest wreath of the Christmas season! Have the whole family help with the baking.

Make a recipe of roll-out cookie dough (page 8). Divide into four portions and tint each a different bright color by kneading in liquid food color. Keep portions well wrapped in plastic until ready to roll out. Roll out and cut with a star cookie cutter, then cut a hole in a point of each star with tube 6 for hanging. Bake and cool. String pieces of florists' wire through holes and twist wires onto branches of an artificial wreath. Spectacular!

Follow a star

Bring the Christmas story of the three kings to life on a star-shaped cake.

1. Decorate the kings first. They're trimmed with hard-drying royal icing, so the children can save them. Paint three ice cream cones with thinned icing and dry. Cut an "X" on the bottoms of three marshmallows, insert toothpicks then dip in thinned royal icing and dry. Remove picks and gently push a marshmallow onto the point of each cone.

Use your imagination to give each king a different costume. We used tube 2 to pipe features, hair, beard and mustaches. Lightly mark outlines of full sleeves on cones and fill with tube 13 stars. Add more stars for rounded look. Hands are done with tube 4 shell shapes.

The white haired king wears a crown piped with a tube 4B star, edged with tube 13 points. Trim the robe with tube 4 dots and beading.

The king to his left has tube 233 "fur" trim on his robe and a tube 15 collar. The third king wears a robe hemmed with tube 13 stars in a scallop pattern. The same tube pipes his collar. Attach gum drops to the kings' hands.

2. Bake a two-layer star cake. Fill, ice and place on a serving tray. The decorating's easy. Pipe reverse shell borders, tube 19 on bottom, tube 18 on top. Trim sides with tube 17 star-shaped flowers. Set kings on cake top and light the scene with tall tapers. Serve to ten.

Starry night

Reindeer riders

Gay little elves tend Santa's steeds on a loaf cake. The cute figures are quickly created with marshmallows.

1. Make marshmallow elves first. Arms and legs are each formed of two miniature marshmallows, bodies and heads are regular size marshmallows. Thread these separate parts on bamboo skewers (purchase at meat counter), dip in thinned royal icing and dry by sticking skewers into a styrofoam block. Fasten the parts together with the protruding skewers, add ruffly tube 14 collars and tube 4B stars for caps. Do hair and features with tube 2. Attach a tiny ribbon bow to each collar with icing. Press miniature marshmallows on caps.

Secure elf on reindeer's back to reindeer with icing before attaching his legs.

2. Now make reindeer. Dip a miniature marshmallow for each hoof in brown thinned icing. When dry, form each leg by threading four small marshmallows on each hoof with skewers. Make bodies from two marshmallows, clip off a piece of marshmallow and attach for tail, and fasten legs to bodies. Add a small marshmallow nose to half of a regular size one for head, flatten marshmallow pieces for ears and attach, then secure neck to head. Twist florists' wire into 1½" circles for wreaths and pipe tube 65 leaves. Attach ribbon bows and secure to reindeer with a little icing. Now put assembled necks and heads on bodies. Complete with tube 2 eyes and noses.

3. Bake a Long Loaf cake, swirl with boiled icing and set on cake board. Push miniature marshmallows into base of cake for border. Mark sides and corners with a 2¼" round cutter and pipe wreaths with tube 65. Add bows, set figures on top and serve to 16.

Merry Christmas!

Say it again and again on this sweet cake lit with piped candles.

1. Bake, fill and ice a two-layer 10" round cake. Set on tray and lightly mark top with an 8" cake circle. Pipe greeting with tube 2, top and base borders with tube 16.

2. Divide cake side into twelfths and pipe a tube 4B candle at each division. Color-stripe a decorating cone with orange, fill with yellow icing and pipe tube 20 flames. Now swing a garland from candle to candle with tube 233. Do the wreath in center of cake with same tube. Serves 14.

Trim a little tree

Set a candy tree on a candy-trimmed cake to bring joy to the children!

1. Circle an ice cream cone with spearmint leaves, starting at the base and attaching each with royal icing.

2. Bake a two-layer 8" cake, fill and swirl on boiled icing. Pipe base ball border with tube 11, top border with tube 9. Trim sides of cake with fanciful candy flowers. The center of each is a small gumdrop surrounded by cinnamon candies and petals made from slices of large gumdrops. Serve this Sugar Plum cake to ten.

Send love for Christmas

Just a little time is needed to decorate this love-shaped cake trimmed with a glittering Christmas tree.

1. Bake, fill and ice a two-layer 9" heart cake. Transfer *Celebrate!* V pattern to cake top. Outline with tube 2 and a mixture of half piping gel—half royal icing. Combine tinted gel with an equal amount of water and fill in the areas. Trim with cinnamon candies.

2. Drop double tube 13 strings from top of cake and pipe tube 18 rosette borders. This centerpiece serves twelve.

Quick & clever holiday treats
Make one for a special friend, or for a surprise for the youngsters

Make a Christmas wreath... lovely symbol of the season

A flowery wreath

Pastel flowers and fluttering butterflies light up your home at Christmas — but you'll bring this lovely wreath out all through the year. It's made of gum paste to last for years.

1. Make gum paste as described on page 13 and tint. Roll out about 1/16" thick, then cut flower and ivy shapes using cutters from Flower Garden set. Dry on a flat surface. Cut six butterflies with Cookie Party cutter and dry within a small curved surface. Cut flower centers with forget-me-not cutter and round tubes. Attach to flowers while still wet with egg white. Cut designs for butterflies with tubes. Attach while wet with egg white. Secure florists' wire to the back of one butterfly with wet gum paste brushed with egg white.

2. Cut wreath frame from a 12" circle of 1" thick styrofoam and remove a 10" circle from the center. Paint with thinned royal icing and dry. Put a piece of wire through top for hanging and twist into loop. Cut a 38" long, 3½" wide strip of green gum paste. Brush wreath with egg white and smooth strip over wreath, leaving loop uncovered. Thread ribbon through loop.

3. Now assemble the wreath. To attach all pieces, roll a little ball of wet gum paste, brush with egg white, press on back of piece, brush again and attach piece to wreath. First attach leaves, then flowers and finally butterflies. Push wire on the one butterfly into wreath frame. Dry. Spray with several coats of clear acrylic spray.

A holly wreath

A scarlet cardinal perches on a spray of holly. Create this outstanding cake for your nicest holiday party.

1. Figure pipe cardinal with royal icing and *Celebrate! V* pattern. Use tube 6 to build up shape of bird. Dry.
Gently pipe feathers with tube 101s. Begin at lower part of bird and work up. Add texture with a palette knife. Do wing and tail last. Eye and black "mask" are piped with tube 1. Paint ring around eye with thinned icing.

2. Pipe holly with Color Flow technique on squares of wax paper over *Celebrate! V* pattern. Pipe tube 2 center vein, then flow thinned icing almost to edges. Move icing with brush to fill pattern. Dry on and within a curve.

3. Bake a 10" x 4" round, two-layer cake. Fill, ice and place on serving tray. Pipe tube 18 base shell border with tube 14 stars between shells. Pipe tube 18 top shell border. Pipe holly stems with tube 3. Secure leaves with dots of icing, then pipe tube 3 berries. Secure cardinal on mound of icing, then pipe legs with tube 1. Add clusters of holly at base of cake. Serves 14.

1953. *"Our first big success in selling the book (Modern Cake Decorating) was the result of a call on the May Company in Cleveland. The buyer there was very enthusiastic about cake decorating and she got me on a TV show, and put an ad in the newspaper. We gave demonstrations, one in the morning and one in the afternoon for two days in their auditorium. We thought possibly we could sell a thousand books—in those two days we sold two thousand."* —NORMAN WILTON

Deck the halls

Trim a Christmas cake with gingerbread angels and holiday greenery.

1. Make gingerbread using recipe on page 19 or your own favorite. Cut angels with Giant Angel cookie cutter. Cut wreath with a 3" round cutter, remove the center with a 1¾" cutter and lay on angels to bake with them in position. Pipe trims on angels with tube 2 and royal icing. Cover wreath with tube 233 and add tube 3 berries. Dry, then attach a popsicle stick to the back of each angel with royal icing so it extends from the bottom. Dry.

2. Bake a 9" x 13" x 4" two-layer sheet cake. Fill, ice and place on foil-covered cake board. Pipe tube 22 bottom shell border. On top edge, divide long sides of cake into fifths, short sides into thirds. Drop string guidelines from point to point, then pipe tube 17 zigzag garlands covering the guidelines. Trim intersections with a tube 101 bow. Pipe tube 3 lettering on cake side.

3. Push popsicle sticks on angels into cake top. Push three tapers into cake behind angels. Serves 24.

Peace on earth
Quick & clever

Celebrate the birth of the Prince of Peace with this lovely cake topped with a star method plaque.

1. Tape *Celebrate! V* pattern to a flat surface and cover with wax paper. Outline design with tube 1 and royal icing. Fill in faces and background with tube 14 stars. Pipe lion's mane and lamb's wool with tube 14 curved shells. Outline eyes, nose, mouth and insides of ears with tube 1, then fill in with thinned icing. Dry thoroughly, then brush flowed-in areas with corn syrup or piping gel to glaze.

2. Bake an 8" x 4" round, two-layer cake. Fill, ice and place on serving tray. Pipe tube 16 rosette borders at the top and bottom. Pipe tube 2 message on side. Trace star pattern on cake side, outline with tube 1 and fill with tube 14 stars. Secure plaque to cake top on mounds of icing. Serves ten.

The angels' song

Three chubby choir boys sing the angels' song on this Christmas cake.

1. Make four paper cones about 5" high for trees. Cover cones with icing, pipe tube 16 upright shells on them, then cover with tube 76 "needles". Dry. Using *Celebrate! V* star pattern, outline with tube 2 and Color Flow icing, then flow in thinned icing. Dry. Attach to tops of trees with icing.

Pipe tube 67 holly leaves on wax paper and pull out points with damp brush.

2. For choir boys' heads, cover three marshmallows with thinned icing. Bake three small Wonder Mold cakes for bodies. Ice red, then pipe tube 104 ruffle about 1" up from bottom. Fill area between ruffle and top with tube 14 stars. Figure pipe sleeves with tube 12 and add tube 104 cuffs. Pipe hands with tube 6. Cut 1" x 2" songbooks from paper, fold and insert between hands. Add tube 10 shoes. Pipe a tube 10 red ball on top of figures and attach heads with toothpicks. Pipe tube 2 eyes, mouth, ears and hair. Pipe tube 4 cheeks and flatten with damp finger.

3. Bake a 9" x 13" x 4" two-layer sheet cake. Fill, ice and place on a foil-covered cake board. Cut a 7" x 10" oval pattern and transfer to the cake top. Mark a curve on each side of cake near corners. Fill area outside top oval and between marked curves and around corners on cake sides with tube 2, piping small heart shapes that barely touch each other. Outline oval and curves with tube 16 shells. Pipe tube 16 top shell border, tube 18 on bottom.

Attach holly leaves to shorter sides of cake with dots of icing. Pipe tube 3 berries and tube 2 lettering.

4. Attach choir boys to cake top with icing, positioning the trees behind them. Cake serves 24 and three lucky children get the choir boys.

1957. *"People started buying Modern Cake Decorating and then they began to ask where they could buy cake decorating supplies. There was no place a housewife could buy these things at that time. I made up a mail order sheet—about eight pages of cake decorating ideas with a list of tubes, colors, decorating bags, parchment paper and so forth. We started filling the mail orders about twice a week from the basement of our house. We thought we were really streamlined when we acquired a stamp machine! That was our first automation."*—NORMAN WILTON

Carol cakes

The sounds of Christmas! The crunch of footsteps in the snow, the crackle of burning logs, the clang of bells, the sweet poignant lilt of children singing.

Christmas cookie village (shown on page 123)

Here's a holiday project the whole family will have fun creating! All the little structures in this peaceful village are built of purchased cookies and crackers. Caution—it's not edible because the finished scene is sprayed with acrylic so it will last for holidays to come.

1. Your first stop is the supermarket! Buy an assortment of cookies, crackers and candies. Then begin to experiment with assembling buildings for the village. Use royal icing to attach the pieces. Be creative, use your own ideas! If you need to cut the cookies or crackers, use repeated strokes of a sharp knife to prevent shattering. Save the buildings you like and use them as models when assembling the finished village scene.

2. The finished buildings are assembled on supports of 1" thick styrofoam. This gives them strength and makes them much easier to assemble. Measure the insides of the models and cut the styrofoam slightly smaller than the measurements. Attach the walls of the buildings around the supports using royal icing. When the buildings are all assembled and dried, trim them with pieces of candy.

3. For the large tree, make an 8¾" high cone, 3" in diameter at base from light cardboard. Cut spearmint leaves candies to half thickness. Beginning 1" up from base of cone, attach the leaves with icing, overlapping them as you move up. Pipe green icing between them to conceal cone. Secure a gum drop on top. Trim the Christmas tree with cinnamon candies.

4. Cut a 23" circle from ¼" thick plywood for base and cover with foil. Cut a 22" round base from 1" thick styrofoam. Secure styrofoam to foil-covered board with nails. Cut a hole in styrofoam for large tree and mark positions of the buildings. Soften royal icing with a little corn syrup, then ice the styrofoam, bringing the icing to just within the marked areas for the buildings. Place buildings and tree in position, then landscape with gum drop bushes and small trees made with a gum drop on a pretzel stick. Spray one area at a time with clear acrylic spray and quickly sprinkle with edible glitter. When entire scene has been sprayed and sprinkled with glitter, spray again several times to help preserve it.

Store in a large plastic bag in a cool, dry place. Bring it out year after year as a treasured holiday decoration.

1958. *"I was always doing pulled sugar work in my workshop, and this gave me time to get various ideas for products. I would ask the supply houses we bought from to make up different designs for wedding ornaments, tier separators and so forth. They would make them up and then sell them to us. Finally I said, we should be making these things ourselves! I went to the Japanese Trade Center and inquired about a company to make various items for us. We started manufacturing a number of products in Osaka, Japan. That was the start of our overseas operations."*—NORMAN WILTON

Grand Prize Winners

in Celebrate's Jubilee Sheet Cake contest.
A hearty thank you to all of you who entered creative cakes
—well-earned congratulations to the lucky winners.
We've included all patterns needed in the Celebrate! V Pattern Book.

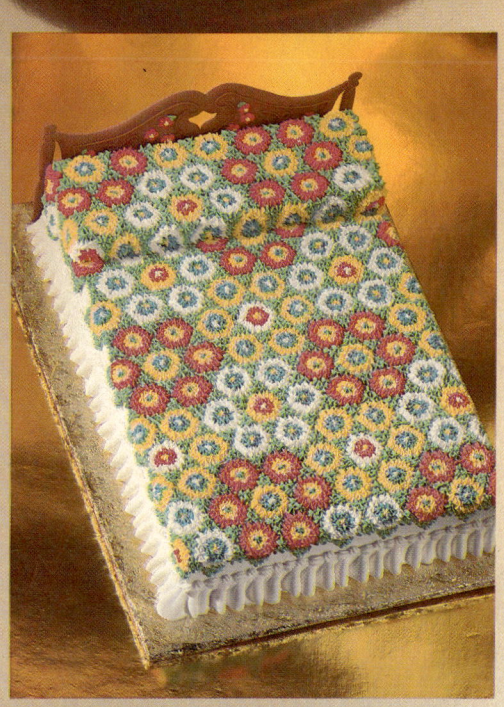

First grand prize, $500 and a 15″ gold-plated tray to Marilyn Butts

Hickory, Dickory, Dock is the most appealing clock cake we've ever seen! Marilyn iced a 9″ x 13″ sheet cake, and then used gum paste to create the handsome clock. The sculptured trim is molded in Baroque molds and Color Flow makes the numbers. The highlights of the cake are two pert little mice. Marilyn figure piped them according to directions in Celebrate! III.

Second grand prize, $300 and a 13″ gold-plated tray to Karen Ramsay

Grandmother's prize quilt, a most ingenious reproduction of a flowery old quilt pattern that covers a 9″ x 13″ sheet cake. Karen formed the pattern of equilateral triangles by carefully drawing horizontal lines every half-inch across the iced cake, then adding diagonal lines. She outlined the areas and then filled in the design with stars. Her pattern-making skill resulted in a quaintly charming prize winner.

Third grand prize, $100 and an 11″ gold-plated tray to Sherry Aremas

Flowers of May is the name of this pretty prize winner. Sherry shows how a simple strong design can set off beautifully piped flowers and stringwork. She neatly divided the top of her 11″ x 15″ cake into diamonds and centered each with a cluster of petunias. Icing loops fill in the corners. Proof again that simplicity is always beautiful.

Winners of $100

in Celebrate's Sugar Plum Birthday Cake Contest.

Our panel of judges debated long and seriously before deciding the winner in each category of birthday cakes—there were hundreds of bright, outstanding entries to consider. Sincere thanks to all of you who shared ideas with us. To each winner, in addition to the cash award, a 24-karat gold-plated cake server, engraved with her name.

To Faye Harrell, $100 and a gold-plated server for her teen's cake

Here's a sure-fire winner for a teen's birthday! Faye has re-created a young girl's favorite entertainment, the slumber party. She starts with the bed—a 14″ square cake cut in half and stacked. Head and footboards are done in Color Flow, the two cute girls are figure piped. Records are plastic.

To Denise Watkins, $100 and a gold-plated server for her child's cake

Have you ever seen a cuter cowboy? Denise made him from two cakes baked in the horseshoe pan, two 9″ x 13″ sheet cakes and an 8″ round cake. Here is a really creative use of pans! Decorating is simple and colorful. Round up all the children in the neighborhood for the birthday party— this cowboy cake is really tall!

To Helen Siskosky, $100 and a gold-plated server for her man's cake

Happy Sails is a really impressive birthday tribute to a man! Just as impressive is Helen's inventiveness in creating this three-dimensional ship in gum paste. She used the Color Flow pattern for the "Flying Cloud" in *Celebrate! II Pattern Book*. The sails were dried in curved forms and rigged on dowel rod masts. Helen covered the sides of the 10″ cake with chopped nuts. We suggest setting the ship on a separator plate to be lifted off before serving—it's too handsome not to save!

A $50 Wilton gift certificate to each of these Jubilee Sheet Cake winners!

A lively imagination and skillful use of tubes made these four cakes winners! We only wish there could be a prize for every entry—our readers demonstrated that simple sheet cakes can be real works of art!

A golden butterfly
Joan Schield shows how daintly piped lattice can create an outstanding cake. She piped the large butterfly right on the 11" x 15" cake, the smaller butterflies at the corners over patterns, and then assembled them after drying. The curved lattice lines on the sides of the cake display tiny "peek-a-boo" roses. *Joan Schield* has created a little masterpiece to star at a shower, an announcement party or any feminine get-together.

Mother hen tells the news
Susan Muzzy created a 9" x 13" baby shower cake that shows a sense of humor. The hen's body is piped with a leaf tube to create a feathery, soft look. The other areas of the design are filled in with star tubes.

A hand-crafted baby blanket
Nancy Neal shows her special technique for creating a crocheted and knitted cake top on this adorable 12" x 18" baby cake. The blanket is piped with round tubes. The darling teddy bear is formed with marshmallows, assembled with toothpicks and covered with stars for a fluffy look. Nancy Neal has created a showpiece cake for a shower, birth announcement party, for baby's first birthday or christening.

A blooming window
Judith Gariepy and *Deborah O'Connor* collaborated on this beautifully designed 12" x 18" cake. It proves that realistic flowers and plants can be produced using tubes and a little imagination. This cake is the perfect tribute to a plant lover on any occasion.

More clever Jubilee Sheet Cake winners!

Unusual designs plus interesting techniques add up to prize-winning cakes. We're happy to award each winner a $50 Wilton gift certificate.

A jolly scarecrow
Edna Kirby combines techniques on this happy 9" x 13" cake. She pipes tube 199 pumpkins trimmed with vines and leaves for the base border, and adds more on top of the cake. Golden mums trim the cake corners. She painted a sugar mold scarecrow for the centerpiece with thinned icing. Edna created this colorful cake for a birthday, but it would be just as much fun to make for Halloween.

A dainty baby buggy
Lucille Ferguson creates the delicate buggy on this stunning cake with nylon netting, royal icing and tube 1. She uses it, plus daisies, roses and kneeling angels with cornelli robes to trim an 11" x 15" cake. What a beautiful baby shower cake! The buggy is a lovely keepsake for the new mother.

A vivid aquarium
James Goddard trimmed a 12" x 18" cake with colorful piped tropical fish, using tubes 104, 102 and 2 to create them. They look so realistic! He created the textured background by spreading the icing with a spatula. *James Goddard* has created a fantastic cake any tropical fish lover will adore!

Butterflies and flowers
Jeane Kennedy welcomes spring with this fresh, lovely 11" x 15" cake. It is well-designed and executed, with a beautiful air of simplicity. The butterfly is piped of lattice and stars in an openwork design, then the cake is trimmed with daisies. This is an attractive cake for almost any occasion.

Congratulations and a $50 gift certificate to each

Pastel icing, dainty decorating and bright ideas mark these four prize-winners. They'll inspire you to create your own masterpiece sheet cakes.

Eyelet ruffles trim a cake
Diane Gibbs created a beautiful 11" x 15" baby shower cake with a delicate air. The eyelet ruffles around the sides are the news. Diane piped them with tube 127R, let the icing set up a few moments, then made the holes with a toothpick. Crystal Clear booties are posed in a field of flowers.

Handmade knits for baby
Mary Gamble displays her "knitting" technique on this 12" x 18" shower cake. The balls of yarn are piped with tube 4 over mounds of icing with icing-covered toothpicks for knitting needles. The sweet little baby clothes are done with tube 14 stars. Sweet peas and piped toys, pacifiers and pins finish the cake. Pink and blue question marks top the elongated base border shells.

A toast to the 21st
Carole Gathmann sets a glass of champagne on this 11" x 15" cake for a 21st birthday. She marked the cake top with a 9" petal pan. The champagne glass is outlined, then filled in with sparkling piping gel. Ruffles, cornelli lace and drop flowers complete the cake.

A lacy four-poster
Myrna Scholl starts with a 12" x 18" two-layer sheet cake, adds four 10¼" Roman columns, tops the "posts" with a lacy canopy and creates a most realistic four-post bed! She cut a 1" slice from the 12" side of the cake to form pillows, then covered the entire top of the cake with a lattice design. Myrna made her canopy frame by shaping coat-hanger wires, but you may find it easier to cut the frame from 1" thick styrofoam.

These bright cakes each won a $50 Wilton gift certificate

These four Jubilee Sheet Cake contest winners display our readers' talents in decorating cakes that appeal to special interests. Each uses strong colors in an attractive way.

Dirt rider
Alfredo Marr poses a dramatic Color Flow figure on a 9" x 13" sheet cake done for a birthday. The top border is done with tube 7 balls to reinforce the wheels theme. This cake will appeal to all motorcycle owners. We recommend that popsicle sticks be fastened to the back of the Color Flow piece to be inserted into the cake and help hold it.

A change of scenery
Donna Zieger creates a four-level, dimensional scene in Color Flow and frames it in woodgrain Color Flow. Even the sides of the 12" x 18" cake are covered with "wood" Color Flow panels. Rows of carefully tinted balls build up the levels and help support the frame. Donna writes, "this cake is my demonstration of what can be done with Color Flow and the use of colors."

A vivid Autumn cake
Linda Johnson uses several pans and lots of color to create this harvest scene on an 11" x 15" sheet cake. The pumpkin is baked in the interchangeable ring pan, using only 1½ cups of batter, then covered with stars. Richly tinted stars fill in the leaf shapes and the ears of corn are baked in a corn bread stick pan, then covered with tube 353 kernels. Linda added piped acorns to complete a brilliant cake.

A cake for a swim team party
Kathryn Suess puts the Small Doll picks to an entirely new use—to represent opposing teams of swimmers on a 12" x 18" cake. "Our team is winning of course." Each starting block is made of two sugar cubes, poles are tinkertoy sticks and flags are cut from paper.

More creative winners in the Jubilee Sheet Cake contest

These four winners show how a decorated cake can set the theme for a party—with clever planning and design by the decorator.

The story of a marriage

Pam Laurinas decorated a memorable anniversary cake that shows the highlights of the couple's wedded years. This is a really big cake—two 12" x 18" set side by side. Pam divided the cake, then neatly piped the four homes the couple occupied, three sets of booties to represent the births of their children, the wedding of their son, engagement of the second son, birth of a grandchild and, of course, pictures of the happy couple themselves!

Splash party!

Mrs. D. B. Smith sets a 6" "swimming pool" on an 11" x 15" cake, adds a tree with a styrofoam ball top and populates the scene with little cookie people. This ingenious cake was served for her son's party after the children had had a swim. We know any child would love it!

Christmas greetings

Cora Graham gives an 11" x 15" sheet cake a most professional look by her skillfull decorating. The fat candles are done in a spiral effect with tube 4B. Color Flow makes the dainty holly leaves and the message is piped with a two-color effect by striping a cone fitted with tube 13. A simple, elegant and beautifully done prize winner.

An antique car

Barbara Dinger decorated a very personal cake for her son's 18th birthday. Her son originally drew the sketch of the car. Barbara skillfully transferred the sketch to the cake top, then piped it with a combination of star method and line work. Simple shell borders complete the 11" x 15" sheet cake. We're sure that Scott was delighted with his unique cake!

Two stunning winners in Celebrate's Jubilee Sheet Cake contest

These outstanding cakes show how skilfull decorating and good design can turn a sheet cake into a work of art. Each has an interesting "picture" quality, well suited to the rectangular shape of the sheet cake.

A cake for a sailor

Judith Thompson creates a spirited sailing ship on an 11" x 15" cake. Judith iced the cake in white buttercream, then sprayed it with blue-tinted water from a plant mister. Light blotting with paper towels creates clouds. The hull is done freehand in Color Flow, waves are piping gel and the sails and rigging are piped with tube 2.

Poinsettias in a frame

David O'Malley's wife, Suzanne sent in his entry and explained that David started decorating just recently. His two-layer 12" x 18" cake shows real design ability and careful work. Royal icing poinsettias are piped petal by petal, then assembled. The frame is done in Color Flow and set on sugar cubes. Trim with Color Flow holly.

Jubilee! A sparkling anniversary cake *shown on title page*

The glitter of pulled sugar and the shine of poured fondant come together on a cake for a really big celebration. We regret that space doesn't permit us to print the recipe and directions for the pulled sugar trims, but complete information is in *The Wilton Way of Cake Decorating, Volume II,* as well as in *Celebrate! IV*. If you haven't tried pulled sugar work before, this is a good cake to start on. You'll need only a half-recipe of the candy.

1. Make roses, leaves and bows of pulled sugar. Twist a little of the sugar into a slender rope and form it into the numerals. Glue plates from two petite ornament bases to a 3" Grecian pillar. When the numerals have completely cooled, attach to top plate on a plaque of sugar. Add a few pulled sugar leaves.

2. Bake the tiers. Top tier is an 8" x 2" single round layer plus an 8" bevel layer, filled and iced in buttercream. Base tier consists of two 12" round layers, filled, to a total height of 3". A circle of dowel rods, clipped level with top is inserted, then an 8" separator plate from Crystal Clear set is placed on top. Above this is a 12" top bevel layer. Ice completed tier in buttercream.

Bake a 16" base bevel layer, ice in buttercream and insert dowel rods for support. Place a 10" separator plate on top.

3. Cover base bevel and two tiers with Quick Poured Fondant (page 159). This shiny coating is grease free and will not break down the pulled sugar trim. Cover bevel and tiers separately. Assemble on cake board with 8" separator plate and Crystal Clear pillars. Push pegs down into lower tier until they rest on the separator plate below 12" top bevel layer. Pipe tube 17 shell borders. Set ornament on top, securing with icing, and trim cake with pulled sugar roses and leaves. A shining triumph that serves about 162 guests. (Cut 16" base bevel, 12" round layers and 12" top bevel layer separately.)

Tips from the Celebrate! staff

Always mount cakes on cardboard cake circles or on cardboard cake bases cut to fit. This goes for cake tiers too. Just put a few strokes of stiff royal icing or corn syrup on the cake circle and place the bottom layer of the cake on it, then fill and ice. The cakes are much easier to move, serving trays or separator plates are not scratched when the cake is cut, tiers are easier to assemble. Borders hide the cardboard.

For even layers in a torte, set a large serrated knife on the counter next to the cake. Saw through the cake without lifting the knife. Layers will be beautifully even and just the thickness of the knife handle.

Always chill cake layers before filling and icing. They're much firmer and easier to handle. Freezing is fine too. Allow frozen layers to set, uncovered, at room temperature for about two hours to thaw. Pat with paper towels before icing.

Decorating for Profit

Many thanks to all of you who generously shared your experience. To the writers of each letter printed here, we are sending a $10.00 Wilton gift certificate and our compliments. If the same or very similar advice was submitted, we have printed the entry with the earliest postmark.

Getting started

"Many Americans live here in Stuttgart, and the need for fancy cakes is overwhelming. A local boutique asked me to display my talents in their shop. The shop displays some of my cake pictures and a decorated dummy cake. I change these periodically. The manager takes the name and phone number of anyone who inquires, I contact the person and discuss cake themes. The boutique adds 10% to my fee." *Diana L. McCrary,* Stuttgart, Germany.

"I started decorating for everyone's birthday. I took cakes to church potlucks, bake sales or wherever you could donate baked goods. Soon I had orders coming in. If a hostess asks you to decorate a cake if she provides the supplies—refuse the supplies. This gets you into the profits. Within a year you'll be doing cakes often." *Amy Joan Whitehead,* Highland, CA.

"I guess the one thing that has enabled me to sell some 50-odd cakes and gross over $400.00 in a year is to give away cakes. Take a pretty cake to a church get-together, surprise a neighbor with a birthday cake, dazzle the gang at work with a decorated Easter egg cake. Before long, these people and their friends will order cakes. If I didn't haul hay, and do other farm wife chores or prepare taxes during the tax season, I could probably make a lot of money—but then it would be work, not fun." *Mrs. Kenneth Carr,* Springfield, MO.

"Whenever we have a band carnival, boy scout banquet or church function, I try to make an extra-special decorated cake. When a couple announces their engagement, I send them my card, telling them I bake wedding and shower cakes. I attach gold stickers with my name, address and phone number to all of my cake boxes." *Jan Reynolds,* Centralia, MO.

"At age 15, my mother bought me a basic decorating kit and Wilton Yearbook. I followed the lessons one by one till I had everything down pat. Now I'm 20, a full-time secretary and on the side I do all types of cakes, including wedding cakes. I hope to have a full-time business soon." *Debra Hiers,* Chiefland, FL.

Advertise your talents

"I send wedding cake price lists to all girls announcing their engagement in the paper. At stores' grand openings, I make a special cake and present it to them. I present the first baby of the year with a certificate good for his first birthday cake. It's amazing how many orders one or two free cakes will bring." *Moni Hourt,* Crawford, NE.

"One of the best places to advertise is the local beauty shop. I also go to restaurants and offer 5" or 6" birthday cakes for $1.50. When my freezer gets over-full, I have an 'Everyday Cake Sale'—cakes just frosted for $2.00 to $5.00." *Lorraine Carder,* Packwood, WA.

"Besides putting an ad in the paper each spring, I donate a cake to each high school grade to sell chances on—give birthday cakes to local business men—present birthday cakes to my children's teachers." *Mrs. Daniel Pritchard,* Spalding, NE.

"Advertising in our small town newspaper didn't get me as many customers as doing birthday cakes for the nursing home's monthly party. If the advertising weren't enough, the excitement of the residents would be!" *Jeanne Donley,* Bassett, NE.

"I've found that my own work is my best reference. When interviewing prospective brides, I suggest different cake designs, following the wedding color scheme, using the same type and color of flowers, and up to seven flavors of cake. I ask for the name of the wedding photographer and request a picture of the cake at my expense for my album. I also keep a list of free items available for weddings at various stores, where to buy punch concentrate, how to use colored sheets to drape the tables, list of caterers, etc. Many brides appreciate my tips." *Mrs. J. E. Mushrush,* Hartstown, PA.

"As my main interest is in wedding cakes and I plan to branch out into catering, I send a hand-signed letter to engaged girls telling them the possibilities of design and color for their cakes and inviting them to call me. I enclose my business card. The system has paid off in getting the word out that I'm a good decorator, really interested in them!" *Diane K. Hottle,* Needham, MA.

"First get business cards printed with something a little 'catchy'. (Mine says 'Special Cakes for Special People'.) I found out the birthdays of a favorite waitress, beauty operator, checker, doctor, nurse—and delivered a beautiful cake to them when lots of people were present to admire it. I just leave cards, the orders roll in." *Candy Cartledge,* Des Plaines, IL.

"To give extra service to our regular customers, we keep a file of the names of their family members, birthdays, anniversaries, favorite colors, hobbies and preferences in flavors of cake and icing. A second file lists by months birthdays, anniversaries and other special occasions. Two or three weeks in advance we call our customers to remind them of the occasion coming up. We also keep a notebook describing cakes done, date and price. The biggest work is getting the system set up. It has increased our business and customers love this service." *Rita and Allen Odom,* San Antonio, TX.

Pictures are important

"I only advertise by word of mouth—business is great! If you'd like to do more wedding cakes, give a free two-layer heart cake to the couple. Have a professional photographer take pictures of your cakes—he may increase your business." *Lynda J. Phillips,* Aurora, IL.

"When my cake is completed, I take three 35mm pictures of it—one for my wallet, one for my album and one for the customer. I write my name, address and phone on the back of this one and mail it to the customer after the event. This has gotten me many orders. A second tip—I have as many as 20 pictures printed in a montage on a postcard-sized card. It's much easier to carry or send." *Stella Pyrtek,* Fords, NJ.

"I took an album of pictures of my cakes to an interview at our high school. I was awarded the job of cake decorating instructor at $8.00 an hour. It fulfilled one of my ambitions!" *Jean P. Gallant,* Rumford, ME.

Decorating gives many rewards

"I first decorated three years ago by making a storybook doll cake for my daughter's first birthday. Then I studied *The Wilton Way of Cake Decorating,* and took a night course. Now I teach two classes a week, do some decorating in my home and earn top pay decorating cakes for a local bakery! *The Wilton Way* really paid off for me!" *Brenda Tuntland,* Spanaway, WA.

"With many ladies taking classes at stores and shops, the market will soon be flooded with decorators, so the secret is to have the best cake and best decorating if you want to stay in business. With all the work, love and care that goes into a cake, I often wonder is there really a profit in cake decorating? I find most satisfaction in having created a work of art that pleases someone." *Wanda Johnson,* Indianapolis, IN.

"Decorating is something you can do at

Continued on page 148

"Nifty fifty" decorating tips from our readers

In response to *Celebrate!*'s request for tips on making decorating easier and more fun, we received an avalanche of good suggestions from decorators everywhere. If the same or a similar tip was sent in by several readers, we printed the one with the earliest postmark. We thank all who contributed proven tips and award each winner a $10.00 Wilton gift certificate.

Preparing the cake

"I found a great recipe to release cakes from pans. Mix 3 tablespoons flour, 3 tablespoons cornstarch and 8 tablespoons Crisco. Blend well and store covered in the refrigerator. The mixture will keep for up to one full year." *Mrs. Lynn Hegeman*

"When using a cake mix I double the number of eggs called for and use milk instead of water. This provides extra volume and a taller cake." *Jeanne Donley*

"Need both hands to fill a decorating bag? Take a tall glass, put bag inside with tip down. Turn bag down on top of glass and you have hands free. A small spatula or spoon works best." *Mrs. W. C. Woods*

"To eliminate the crumbs before frosting a cake, first cool cake on a rack and put wax paper over it. Then place a wet terry cloth dish towel (wrung out by hand) over the wax paper. Let set at least 3 hours or overnight. The crumbs will be absorbed into the cake." *Mrs. Jack A. Flynn*

"To transport a cake any distance I use a piece of ¼" plywood, instead of a cardboard base. I cover this with fancy paper or a patterned paper table cover and then with clear contact paper." *Eleanor Rodgers*

"After my cake is baked, instead of sealing it with thinned buttercream, I mix 10X sugar with water to a medium thin consistency, then brush this on the top and sides. This dries to a solid glaze. When I put buttercream over it not a crumb moves to spoil the final icing." *June L. Atkinson*

How to get level cakes

"Here's an easy way to get layers level. Bake layers, then let them cool in the pans. Using pan edge as a guide, slice off the extra with an electric knife. For biggest layers, put pan on a turntable, pile books to the height of the pan edge, and hold the knife on the books. Then turn pan to level the cake." *Diane K. Hottle*

"When I baked at the temperature given on the cake box, my cakes were rounded so I had to cut some off. But if I bake at 300° cakes come out flat on top. It takes ten minutes longer, but I have pretty cakes and they are real moist." *Dianna McCallister*

"To insure a level cake I shake the cake pan after I pour in the batter so it is level. When it is baked I let it stay in the pan for five minutes. Then I turn the pan over, leaving it on the cake, with a weight on it, five minutes more. When I take the pan off, the cake is completely level." *Penni Panarello*

"If you add one extra egg to your cake batter (one egg white if a white cake) and turn the temperature down 25 degrees, the cakes come out very flat." *Jackie Kroeker*

"When a cake comes out of the oven and it's rounded on the top, I put a clean towel on the top and press lightly to make a flat top." *Yvonne J. Carrabine*

"For my large cakes I take a piece of aluminum foil larger than the pan, then take wet paper towels and fold to fit the side of the pan, all around the sides. I then fold the foil over the wet paper up to the top of the pan. I bake my cakes at 300°." *Ida Mae Tankersley*

Ed. note: many decorators attested to the success of wrapping a wet terry cloth strip around the pan during baking, a suggestion previously made in Wilton publications.

Better icings, better decorating

"When I don't have time to sift the confectioners' sugar for icing I put it in a bowl and at high speed use the electric mixer for a minute. It does a good job." *Sandy Morgan*

"For deep red buttercream, try this. Tint your frosting pale orange first. Then add red paste color and let the frosting set. The longer it sets the darker it gets." *Joyce Bos*

"I use this variation of the Buttercream recipe for making flowers and borders when the weather is humid. To basic recipe add 1 cup shortening, 2 tablespoons cornstarch and substitute 1 or 2 large egg whites for the milk. If icing is too stiff, beat in extra egg white; if it is too soft add powdered sugar. I chill the flowers before putting them on cake." *Brenda Lae*

"To make buttercream hold its shape better, I add ½ to 1 cup of powdered milk to the Wilton recipe, first mixing this with the milk or cream required to avoid a grainy texture. A big help." *Denise Rodgers*

"My family doesn't like super sweet frostings. I add a slight amount of Imitation Rum flavoring to all my frostings. It cuts the 'sweet' taste." *Merrie A. Sprague*

"When decorating a cake I can make it very 'personal' with a Color Flow icing decoration. Because Color Flow softens after a while when placed on buttercream icing, I make the Color Flow decoration on wax paper, and then later cut around it with a razor blade so paper backing remains. This keeps the decoration from softening. It can be later lifted off for a gift to the 'guest of honor'." *Martha Munoz*

Making better tier cakes

"Before placing my separator plate on the top of a frosted layer, I place plastic wrap on top of the frosting, making certain that the wrap is completely concealed. When the caterer removes the cake for cutting, the plate comes off clean and plastic wrap is easily removed." *Hazel K. Derstler*

"A wedding cake can be beautiful until it comes time to cut it. Then the bottom separator plate frequently pulls icing up with it. Sprinkle a thin layer of coconut under the separator plate and it will lift off easily for cutting." *Lorraine Von Hofen*

"I use plastic straws (instead of wooden dowels) for the support of tiers when I make multi-tier wedding or anniversary cakes. They are always clean, easier to obtain and are easier to cut." *Carol R. Young*

Ed. note: This would work well on smaller cakes, but be cautious on large cakes!

"Wedding cakes are easier to work with if tiers are frosted and filled while frozen. Cover with plastic and let set overnight to thaw. The next day frost again. First frosting will be set and second frosting will go on smoothly. Cut circle of plastic wrap the size of cake separator plate, fasten in pegs through plastic wrap and push separator and plastic undersheet onto cake tier. This prevents frosting from being pulled off when separator is removed. The *extra* coat of icing corrects cracks from cake settling when thawing and keeps cake from cracking when moved. In all the hundreds of wedding cakes I have made I never had one crack during delivery." *Mrs. J. E. Mushrush*

Make decorating easier

"To save frosting and build a sturdy rose, I build my roses on marshmallows. The guests love the taste, too." *Lina LoBasso*

"Being a 'beginner' at decorating, I am slow! To eliminate the panic, I start flowers as soon as I get the order. After arranging them on a plastic-covered dummy of the proper size, I can lift a spray into place on my iced and bordered cake in seconds. By making extras, a break is no catastrophe. Unused extras go into the 'bank' for instant cakes we often need." *Robbie Silver*

"To avoid throwing away any leftover dabs of icing, I make fall leaves. A cornucopia or basket of leaves is beautiful. If it is not fall, I make a batch of ice cream cone cakes. (Simple cake batter in regular flat bottom ice cream cones.) When finished, I frost with all my dabs of icing. Use any large star tube to make 'ice cream' swirl." *Bonnie Kovatch*

"I have a lazy susan with a turntable base. When doing cakes I use the turntable base to hold the cake. I find it easier, as I can turn it without being afraid I might stick my finger in a border." *Marilyn Myers*

"I found this idea comes in handy when you need just a small amount of icing such as for eyes on Sesame Street character cookies. Put a plastic sandwich bag over your hand, fill the tube you are going to use with frosting and use your finger to force out the frosting." *Kathryn M. Pushor*

"As a long time quiltmaker, I have a large collection of quilt patterns. The applique patterns are excellent for reproducing on a cake. The animals on baby quilts make cute children's cakes. Use star fill-in technique or Color Flow." *Jane Moore*

"I use colored glass-head pins to mark divisions on cakes. The pins are highly visible, make it easy to see if divisions are even and they're easy to move. Stringwork can be dropped without moving them and the holes left behind are invisible. They're cheap and washable, too." *Adela Leger*

"Practice on the back of a sheet pan and you'll have a better cake. And Wilton cake decorating supplies are very handy. I'm only twelve years old and have at least $50 worth. To tell the truth, I don't think I could do it without Wilton." *Marianne Austin*

Some real time-savers

"When I'm doing flowers using the lily nail and royal icing I put the flower with the foil around it in a 200° oven for five minutes and it speeds up drying." *Christine Moody*

"When making daisies or roses the Philippine way, I found my daisies were easier to work with if I pushed a square of wax paper up the stem and then piped on my petals. Flowers can then be placed right side up on the rack, with the stem hanging. This curves the daisy petals either up or down, depending on the way the wax paper curls." *Deanna Bowersox*

"After making flowers in the two-piece lily nails, I can remove them easily by lifting them out by the foil and placing foil and frosting flower into freezer 10 to 15 minutes. They come out easily and can be placed on the cake earlier." *Mrs. Robert Hansen*

"After I finish decorating, I use my leftover icing to make flowers. I can usually get four or five roses, or a dozen or so drop flowers. If buttercream, I put them in a tin pie plate and invert another on top, staple all around, and freeze. If royal icing, they are simply dried, put in a box and put on my shelf. This way I never have to throw out any icing. Soon you'll have a supply of flowers for an emergency." *Lynne Freeman*

"A quick, attractive and inexpensive dessert for 'drop-ins' is achieved by topping ice cream with buttercream flowers made from leftover icings, frozen and stored in a plastic container. You have a flower garden of special desserts." *Tosca Sorci*

"When decorating I always have a sink full of hot water for cleaning my tubes and bags. For most people, this is true, but when one lives in the 'bush' [Ed. note: Alaska], hauls water and has to heat it by the wood stove, one gives more thought to cleaning." *Sandra Everly*

"Something I find helpful is to take a small jar and put warm water in to clean tubes as I go. If it's a pint jar, about half full is plenty. Then I add a good grease-cutting dish soap and when I've finished using a tube I drop it in the jar. After I shake the jar, the tubes are nearly clean. Finally, I rinse them and dry with Q-tips." *Georgia Moser*

"To store small plastic ornaments, put up a large peg board. Use fold lock type baggies, reinforce a small square at the top with light cardboard and put in an eyelet (like those used in belts). Ornaments can be separated and hung in the bags. They will be dust-free and easy to find." *Rose A. Sutton*

"I am a working mother who loves to bake and decorate cakes, but have little time. I bake and freeze cakes a week or two before they are needed. I devote a few hours every few months to making royal icing flowers to store in airtight containers for future use. Since buttercream is a cinch to make and my cakes and decorations are on hand, I am prepared to enjoy my hobby on short notice." *Mrs. Richard Kraemer*

A few more tips

"I keep graham crackers on hand and let my children decorate them with leftover icing." *Mrs. R. L. Cain*

"The best place I have found to store paste food colors is in the door of my freezer... I've found freezing the colors keeps them moist. When I'm ready to use a color, I take out the jar and leave it at room temperature 10 to 15 minutes." *Melanie Childress*

"When I write or print on a cake, I first write the message in white, using tube 4. I then pipe a colored icing directly on top of the white, using tube 3. This gives a nice 3-D appearance." *Mrs. Kermit Froiland*

"When writing or printing, I have found that the smallest rose tube, 101s, makes a ruffle design. It stands out, and is very attractive for any occasion." *Joyce Wickiser*

"I found that tube 352 makes fantastic, fluffy leaves of any size. The point of the tube is middle of the leaf." *Shari Bahr*

"On children's cakes I find boys and girls enjoy a cake with real toys on top. Matchbox cars, for instance, or Barbie dolls. The added extra makes the cake more important for the child, after he or she decides the cake has to be cut, no matter how nice it would be to keep." *Dawn Van Why*

"I have a 'cake being delivered' sign on the back window of my station wagon... other motorists tend to be more patient, if you drive a little slower to miss those pot holes that can badly jar a cake." *Emma Dinan*

Decorating success stories

"When our boys were in the Service, we didn't want them to feel forgotten on their birthdays. I baked their favorite angelfood, then wrapped the cake and lined the shipping box with plastic wrap. I'd prepare the white or colored butter icing, seal it in a plastic bag and put it in the corner. Next I'd pack popcorn around the cake and enclose candles and a plastic knife. It always arrived in A1 shape!" *Eleanor C. Denlinger*

"When my children were married, they wanted a carrot cake for their wedding reception. And it had to be for 350 people! I found that by working with frozen layers, they were much easier to handle and to frost and decorate. They also wanted it decorated in earth tones, so I used coffee in the water part of the recipe for my decorator icing. It gave it a perfect earthtone. I used fresh flowers on top combining them with fresh wheat we gathered. I then made wheat stalks from icing on the sides of the lower tiers. It was highly effective and exactly what they wanted." *Gladys Nitzberg*

"I started cake decorating in 1961 when I purchased a copy of *Modern Cake Decorating*. My husband is a chaplain in the Army, so I have used my decorating skills for various projects. I don't sell my cakes as a rule. I contribute them for fund raising activities or surprise friends. This year I made 25 panorama eggs and gave them to new chaplains' wives and people who did extra work for chapel programs. I get my sense of satisfaction when something I created helps to bring joy to someone. That's a great feeling." *Sylvia Degi*

"I think I have achieved a special decorating success. I have been a member of a 4-H Club for seven years. I am 16 years old. As a 4-H project I did a 15-minute demonstration on cake decorating, under the division *Sr. Other Foods*. I showed people how to use the correct equipment—how to do borders, lettering, how to make roses. I had two cakes on display. This was a competitive event. I won on the county level, the nine-county area level and finally at the Kentucky State Fair! I am a *Sr. Other Foods* Champion! This was something I had been working for for five years. Thank you for all the great ideas." *Cindy Covington*

Decorating for profit continued

home and make money. I have four small children and a mother who is ill, so I'm here at home with her, doing all my housework and making money at the same time." *Mrs. Daniel Green,* Nashville, TN.

"After nine months of doing cakes for friends and the church, I began to sell cakes. I charge $6.00 for a small sheet cake, $10.00 for a larger one, $8.00 for an oval flower cart cake and 55¢ a serving for a wedding cake. I also give classes, charging $20.00 and $25.00 for a six-week, twelve-hour course. Last year I made $3,000.00. It's great to be home and still earn money!" *Mrs. Tom Kennedy,* Fredericktown, MO.

"My hobby has turned into a source of income, helping my husband and five children. My motto is 'Whatever you do to help others is returned twice over'." *Josephine Myers,* Syracuse, NY.

How much to charge

"For wedding cakes I charge about 30¢ a serving. I also charge book price for the top separator plate—the bride freezes the top tier for her first anniversary. For the remaining plastic pieces—pillars, plates, bells, etc., I charge a rental fee of $10.00 to $20.00." *Sheryl Housner,* Milton, PA.

"I have found pricing by recipe works well. I charge three times the amount of my expenses. I require a deposit of the cost of expenses on all big orders, and a rental fee for separator sets, tablecloths and other items." *Mrs. Larry Joe Birney,* Sublette, KS.

Editors' note: the deposit will solve the problem of canceled orders.

"I charge $5.00 to $8.00 for birthday cakes, 50¢ a serving for wedding cakes, $8.00 to $12.50 for groom's cakes. I give the bride a cake server and a boxed 6" cake, decorated like the wedding cake, ready to freeze. I learned decorating from your books and have sold hundreds of cakes." *Mrs. S. B. Hendrixson,* Porum, OK.

"My cake prices start at $12.00 to $15.00 for a 9" x 13" cake. Most of mine are made from scratch the same day they are picked up. For special work done in advance, royal icing, Color Flow or marzipan, I charge $3.00 extra. To my customers it's worth it." *Pat Post,* Houston, TX.

"I add up my expenses—cost of ingredients for a one-cake mix cake and icing, and minutes of oven and mixer use at the local rate. I double this figure for a simple cake, triple it for a very ornate one." *Robbie Silver,* Talbott, TN.

New ideas

"I put on parties for young children in the nursery school my mother owns. I do the whole party—invitations, favors, games, party hats and refreshments. The centerpiece is always a beautifully decorated cake. I schedule the parties on evenings and weekends when my husband can baby-sit our two children, one and four." *Carol Ferensak,* Bridgeport, CT.

"I keep two-layer 5" cakes on hand and decorate them for a child or senior citizen. I sell them for 75¢ at the Farmer's Market and at our church bazaar. They have really made a hit!" *Cecilia Smith,* Sequim, WA.

"I'm an entertainer! Many women's clubs have found that my decorating demonstrations have greatly boosted attendance at their meetings. I come with an undecorated cake and decorate it before the women, explaining the techniques. Before leaving the cake is auctioned or raffled. I've been asked back many times to the same group—one time I may demonstrate a doll cake, other times a rose spray or child's cake. I charge $25.00 to $35.00." *Shaindel Cohen,* Lakewood, NJ.

"Develop a technique of your own, different from other decorators in your area. No one here is using Color Flow, so I use it whenever I can." *Karen Burkhart,* Pryor, OK.

"Ice cream 'n' cakes are perfect summer party treats. These cakes are two layers, an ice cream layer on the bottom and a cake layer on top, then covered with softened ice cream and frozen overnight. Buttercream adheres well to the frozen surface. Decorating must be simple and well-planned—if you have a chest freezer, the cake can sit inside of it while you work." *Susan Brown,* Shaker Heights, OH.

Make your customers happy

"I make my cakes personally directed for the person for whom the cake is being ordered. I ask for hobbies, occupation, sports, favorite color, etc. and incorporate these ideas in decorating the cake." *Linda Trout,* Seneca Falls, NY.

"I try never to refuse a cake request, even a last-minute one. When I make Color Flow designs, I always make extras. On a slow day, I'll make seasonal designs. They keep indefinitely and really cut my decorating time." *Helen Yeager,* Virginia Beach, VA.

"Gum paste figures are new in my area, and I've received orders for birthday cakes with People Mold figures depicting the 'birthday person' engaged in a favorite hobby or activity." *Jane Lodl,* Madison, TN.

"I ask the bride what type of bouquet she will carry at the wedding. I have a corsage made to match and place it within the pillars of the wedding cake, for the bride to wear on her honeymoon trip." *Carol Oliver,* Provincetown, MA.

"The character cakes are favorites for children's parties and are not obtainable at bakeries. It's easy to keep busy doing only these cakes." *Debra Allen,* Toledo, OR.

"Every once in a while, I'll take a steady customer a free 'anyday' cake to let her know I appreciate her business." *Mrs. R. L. Cain,* Chancellor, AL.

"One of my biggest selling points is delivery of the cake to the customer. I include a small amount in the price of the cake for this service. If the event is more than ten miles from my shop, I charge $10.00." *Mrs. Pat Wood,* Belleview, FL.

Save time, save money

"I mix the cake fragments left over from leveling cakes with buttercream, and use it for filling wedding cakes. If the mixture is too dry, add a little cold water." *Eva Woods,* Newport News, VA.

"Make seasonal trims ahead of time. Last year I made two recipes of Color Flow autumn leaves and used them on everything from a wedding cake to a football banquet cake." *Nancy Beideck,* North Chili, NY.

"Every step done in advance saves valuable time. I bake my cakes ahead, wrap in plastic and freeze. I also make my icing in advance, tint it, and refrigerate tightly covered. Any flowers, gum paste figures or sugar molds can be made as much as ten days ahead." *Melanie Childress,* Hanover, IN.

"When I have small amounts of batter left over I bake it in the Petite Doll Cake Pan and freeze. I can decorate a small doll to set on a girl's cake, a teepee for a boy or use it in lots of other ways." *Connie Richardson,* Bellefontaine, OH.

"Use the Cake Icer tube and a 16" bag to frost sides of round or sheet cakes. For a two-layer cake, run a strip around the side at base first, then add a second strip, overlapping the first by ¼". Pull excess icing onto cake top. Smooth with a spatula dipped in hot water, then ice cake top. This controls the amount of icing on the cake and is much faster." *Judie Newell,* Billerica, MA.

"No matter how small an amount of icing is left over, store it in a plastic container. Place plastic wrap over the container, then put the lid on." *Marion Tomlinson,* Melrose, FL.

Summing it all up

"I hope these ideas will help. I keep a clip board with order blanks by my telephone. I tape a business card on top of my cake boxes and put two extra cards inside. I always give candles to match birthday cakes. I keep all my decorations in clear plastic shoe boxes. I have a box for each category—men, women's, boy's, girl's, graduation, etc. To help customers visualize a wedding cake, I construct one with cake dummies, using separator sets, fountain and flowers. I encourage customers to help design their cakes. I've been decorating since 1971 and I love it!" *Emma Dinan,* Wilmington, DE.

Commonsense

for cake decorators by Norman Wilton

When you ask almost any decorator, experienced or novice, what technique she would like help on, the reply is "uses of tubes"—so I've decided to devote this chapter to discussing tubes.

Of course, this is a big subject, one that you could easily write a book on. Here are some basic ideas on tube uses, broken down into piping borders and piping flowers. Let's begin with borders.

Start with simple shells

There's nothing more basic than a shell in decorating so it's important to learn to pipe shells neatly and accurately. Here we're using large tubes so you can see the work close up.

1. When piping shell borders on the top or base of a cake, hold your tube at a 45° angle, and maintain this angle as you go around the cake. Using tube 8B, touch the tube to the surface and begin to squeeze the cone. As the shell builds up, lift the tube about ½", then lessen your pressure as you come down. Stop all presssure as you pull off to a point. Pipe the next shell on the tail of the first one. Keep a steady rhythm as you pipe the border so all shells are uniform.

2. Dress up the shell border above with a tube 74 frame. Start squeezing the cone about the center of the shell, relax pressure and stop entirely as you tuck the tube under the shell.

3. Now pipe a shell border with tube 6B. Notice how the change of tube makes a different looking shell. Frame the base of the shells with tube 14, using a tight "e" motion.

4. Give a different look to a tube 6B border by adding tube 14 swirls. Squeeze as you start the curve, then lighten pressure as you curve up and around the shell.

5. Pipe a curved, comma-shaped border with tube 6B. The technique is similar to the plain shell, except as the shell builds up, circle to the right as you ease off pressure. Trim the shells with tube 101, using a slightly back-and-forth motion to create the ruffles.

Shell border variations

Here are some ideas on how to dress up a simple shell border. Try them, then dream up your own variations.

1. Pipe a shell border with tube 105, keeping it neat and uniform. Note how this tube creates defined, perfect ridges. Use this as a design element and fill the two topmost ridges on each shell with tube 3 lines in a contrasting color.

2. Now pipe a reverse shell border with tube 105. Do this by letting the shells build up, then swinging to the left, then to the right. Fill the ridges with tube 3 contrasting bulbs, using a back-and-forth movement. This border has sort of a "sea spray" effect.

Star drop borders

Here is another very basic border that every decorator should practice until perfect. When you can combine stars into a border, with each one neat and uniform, you can create almost any number of borders by adding strings, frames and other details. If you are a beginning decorator, practice stars on the back of a pan first.

3. Hold tube 1F straight up, perpendicular to the surface. Squeeze, lifting tube about ½", stop squeezing and pull away. This will break off the star neatly. Make a row of stars, using even pressure for uniform size.

Pipe some little tube 38 drop flowers in royal icing. After they're dry, attach one to each star.

4. Use tube 8B to make a star drop border. Edge it above and below each star with tube 14 and a zigzag motion. Drop a row of tube 4 strings. Add a second, deeper row of strings and finish with tube 65 leaves.

Here are a few tips on string work. Thin the icing a bit so it flows out smoothly. If it's too thin it won't hold together. Be sure to have your work at eye level, so raise your cake or practice pan. Touch the tip of the tube to the cake, squeeze with even pressure and pull straight out. Move the tube over and touch the cake again. Most important—do not move your tube down to follow the string—let gravity make the drop. Practice this until you can drop the strings with a rhythmic, uniform motion, almost like a machine.

Norman Wilton · commonsense for cake decorators

Pipe rope borders

5. Use tube 105 again for a clear-cut rope design. Pipe a shallow "s" shape. Tuck the tube into the second curve of the "s" and pipe another. Continue in this way to form the rope. Now accent the design with tube 3 lines.

Garlands are favorite trims

Every decorator loves garlands—they always make a cake look fluffy and festive. All garlands start with a guideline to keep them even—either a marked curve or a dropped string.

6. First practice simple star tube garlands for the side of a cake. Mark even scallops, points touching, with tube 3. Hold tube 14 perpendicular to the surface. Start a zigzag movement with very light pressure at the point of the scallop. As you approach the center, increase pressure and lift tube slightly. Relax pressure and return to surface as you approach the second point. Drop tube 3 guidelines below these garlands, keeping the points directly below the centers of the garlands above. Pipe the garlands with tube 14 exactly as before.

7. Make a very dressy side border by over-piping the garlands above. Pipe tube 14 curves over the upper garlands. Do the same with the lower garlands, starting and ending each curve with increased pressure and a slight twirl. Pipe tube 65 leaves.

8. Use tube 65 for a ruffled double garland. Mark curves for upper garlands and drop string guidelines for lower garlands. Pipe the garlands with very light pressure at points, heavier in center, jiggling your hand for a rippled effect. Drop tube 2 strings over upper garland, double strings over lower. Attach tube 38 drop flowers.

9. Drop string guidelines for scallops, alternately small and large. Use tube 5 to pipe the garland with a back-and-forth movement. Drop tube 2 strings over the garlands, starting and ending with a twirl. Over-pipe with same tube.

10. A double garland tied with bows. Drop guidelines and pipe the upper garland with tube 14 and an "e" motion. Drop guidelines for lower garland and pipe with tube 101, moving hand back and forth for ruffle. Now trim both garlands with tube 2 string drops and pipe "Italian" bows and streamers.

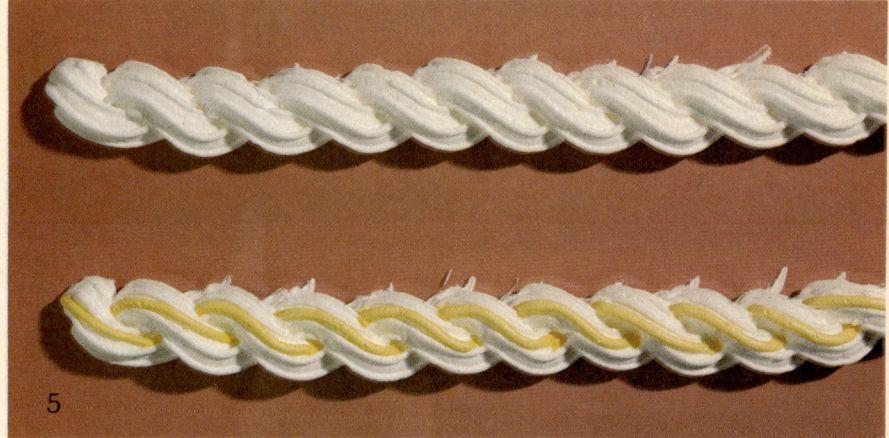

Add charm with flowers

An easy way to create fancy-looking borders is to add drop flowers. Pipe these ahead of time in royal icing. The flowers here were piped with tube 33.

1. With tube 2 and a slight "S" motion, pipe a long curving vine around the cake side. Pipe circles at even intervals within the curves. Pull out short stems and pipe leaves with tube 65s. Now put a little dab of icing on the backs of the flowers and fasten them on the circles.

2 and 3. These borders are similar to the first one. For number 2, I piped leaf shapes in the curves of the vine and filled them with flowers. For number 3, I piped a gull-wing shape, and filled a leaf-shape in center with flowers.

4. Use tube 3 to pipe the garland and drop the strings (see page 151), then pipe a circle above each point of the garland and attach flowers in a wreath.

5. Pipe a curving tube 2 vine around the cake side and within curves pipe clusters of graceful stems. Attach flowers and trim with tube 65s leaves.

6. Pipe tube 3 garlands, just as for number 4 above, and add strings. Add flower arches over the top.

"Sculptured" cake trims

It's a good idea for decorators to have on hand little plastic angel figures or heads. Combine them with curved frames and tiny flowers for wonderful side trims for the big tiers on wedding cakes, or for the top of smaller cakes. All the frames are piped with tube 15.

1. Mark circles on the cake side with a cookie cutter, then make circular motion scrolls. Fasten an Angelino in the center and trim with flowers.

2. Trace triple arch patterns on the side of the cake, outline with "e" motion scrolls, add the angels and tiny roses.

3. Mark half-circles, pipe scrolled outlines and finish with an Angelino and tiny flowers.

4. Cut church-window shapes, transfer to cake and fill in with tube 2 lattice. Attach angels and outline with "e" motion piping. Trim with flowers.

5. Start with a circle, pipe curved scrolls and set in Angelino. Add flowers.

6. Start with the same shape as border 4. Outline with scrolls, add angel and mass flowers at the base.

Piped flowers—always the joy of the decorator

The realism of skilfully piped flowers is really amazing! I think that almost any flower can be duplicated in icing—it just takes observation. All the flowers in this section were done in royal icing. You can make them even months ahead, and they're easy to arrange on a cake or to mount on wire stems.

The Golden Jubilee Rose

These are the blooms that adorn our cover cake and several others in this book. There are only two small changes from piping a regular rose, but they do make a difference.

Have two decorating cones fitted with tube 127 ready. Fill one with deep gold icing, the other with golden yellow.

Attach a square of wax paper to a number 13 flower nail with a dot of icing. With deep gold icing, press out a spiral. Pipe a second tight spiral on top of it. Holding tube almost straight up, wide end down, pipe three upstanding overlapping petals.

Change to golden yellow cone, pipe five petals surrounding the first three, holding tube at slight angle. Add six or seven more petals, holding tube almost horizontal. Dip your fingers in cornstarch and pinch each yellow petal to a furled shape. See how this makes the distinctive Jubilee Rose!

Pipe tube 67 ruffled leaves on wire and bind in clusters of five or three (page 157). For an almost-open Jubilee rosebud, use deep gold icing only.

Dainty morning glories

Line a 1¼" lily nail with foil and use tube 103 and rose colored icing. Place tube deep in nail, wide end down, and pipe a "funnel". Smooth with damp brush. Pipe ruffled edge of flower in one circular movement, lifting hand five times for five-petal effect. Pipe five lines with tube 2 from center of flower to edge, then pull out yellow stamens with tube 1. Lift flower out to dry. When dry, pipe an upstanding tube 10 mound on back and brush to smooth. Pipe calyx with tube 33 and flatten points.

For cake top, pipe a curved tube 2 vine, attach flowers and add tube 67 leaves. For side of cake, omit the tube 10 mound on back and pipe a tube 10 spike to push into cake. See Heavenly Blue morning glories, page 35.

Pipe double spiral and three petals in gold icing
Add five yellow petals
Furl petals

Pipe funnel and smooth
Add five-petal effect
Pipe lines and stamens
Finish back

Commonsense • flowers to assemble on a cake

Here are some unusual flowers to pipe that are done right on the cake. They give a most unusual effect—you'll want to add them to your repertoire.

Fluffy goldenrod
Here's the flower that really gives a fall cake a lot of style. It's piped very simply right on the cake. The block it's shown on here is 3″ high—that gives you an idea of the finished size of the spray.

First pipe a cluster of tube 2 stems, starting on top of the cake and going over the side. Cover the stems with tube 17 elongated shells.

Now cover the shells with tube 13 stars, letting them extend over the surface of the cake. Add a liberal sprinkling of tube 2 dots—the spray is finished. See a goldenrod cake on page 106.

A lilac spray
The lilac is such a favorite of almost everyone, it's a great flower to put on a spring cake. See one on page 63.

Begin by piping many little tube 101s flowers in royal icing, each with four petals. Pipe tube 1s dots in the centers. A quick way to do this is to attach a square of wax paper to a large flower nail and pipe four or five flowers before sliding the paper off the nail to dry.

Now drape a large tube 22 shell over the top edge of the cake. The block this flower is piped on is 3″ high, so you can see the size of the shell. Cover the shell with the little piped flowers, letting them extend out over the cake surface.

Pipe the pointed leaves with slightly thinned icing and tube 352.

154

Commonsense • unusual piped flowers

The "painted" sego lily

Royal icing is used for this flower. Line a 1¼" plastic lily nail with foil. Now pipe a cross with tube 2, letting the ends extend over the edge of the nail. With tube 104, wide end down, pipe three evenly spaced, circular motion petals. Dip your thumb and forefinger in cornstarch and gently pinch the end of each petal to a point.

Let the flower dry a few minutes, then thin paste colors with a little water. Use a fine artist's brush to paint the center yellow and add a red "V" in the center of each petal. Since the sego lily's leaves are threadlike, we have not piped them here.

The red clover, two ways

To pipe this summer flower directly on a cake, buttercream is acceptable. Pipe a tube 12 green bulb, then cover it with tube 1 rosy petals, starting at the top.

To pipe the flower on a wire stem, use royal icing. First prepare the calyx on a wire as shown on page 157. When calyx has dried, pipe a tube 12 mound on it. Now cover mound and calyx with tube 1 petals, starting at top. Pull out green points just below the flower with tube 2. Dry in styrofoam block.

Pipe three heart-shaped leaves with tube 102 on a number 7 nail. Brush center smooth and slide off nail to dry. Attach to the end of a florists' wire with icing, then paint a triangle shape of deep green on each leaf by brushing with thinned paste color. Bind flowers and leaves with floral tape. See page 106 for a pretty clover cake.

The bright bluebonnet

Cover a stiff board with wax paper. Pipe a cupped tube 102 petal, lay the end of a length of florists' wire on the base of it and pipe a second cupped petal slightly overlapping first. Pipe third petal in center by holding tube straight up at base of first two petals. Turn your hand as you squeeze to form an upstanding cupped petal. Pull out a tube 2 white stamen just above this petal. Dry thoroughly.

Pipe long tube 67 leaves on the ends of fine florists' wire. (See page 157.)

When dry, tape together in groups of five. Pipe a dot in center and smooth with brush. Now make a pretty spray by taping flowers and leaves together.

155

Commonsense • favorite flowers for cake trims

Spring's shy violet

No other flower says spring as sweetly as the violet! Turn to page 63 to see how violets turn petits fours into blossoming treats.

Pipe in royal icing. Attach a square of wax paper to a number 7 flower nail. With tube 101, wide end in center, pipe three curved, slightly overlapping petals. Just below this group, pipe two smaller petals, deeply overlapped.

Violet leaves are large. Tape wax paper to a stiff surface. Hold tube 70 in one position, applying steady pressure, until a "V" shape builds up. Decrease pressure, then stop as you draw off to a point. When dry, arrange leaves and flowers into a nosegay. If you wish, you may pipe violet leaves right on the cake, then attach the dried flowers.

The perky pansy

This flower allows the decorator to use deep colors freely. The man's cake on page 86 shows a handsome blending of vivid hues.

Pipe the pansy with tube 124, royal icing and nail number 7. Pipe a curved petal, then a second one, overlapping the first. Repeat with two more petals, right on top of the first pair. Now add a final large ruffled petal, turning your hand to bring it around to the full width of the flowers.

Brush gold icing in the flower's throat. Thin brown paste color and brush the markings on the petals. Arrange flowers on the cake, then pipe ruffled leaves with tube 65.

Pipe a ruffled carnation

Pipe these showy flowers in stiffened royal icing, either on a flower nail or on a wire stem.

Attach a square of wax paper to a number 7 nail and pipe a tube 12 mound of icing. Holding wide end of tube 103 down, and cone parallel with nail, turn nail counterclockwise as you jiggle your hand to produce an upstanding ruffle at top of the mound. Continue adding ruffles, slanting tube outward as you move down mound, until it is completely covered. Slide paper off nail and dry.

To pipe a stemmed carnation, pipe a tube 12 mound on a wired calyx, also piped with tube 12. Hold the stem just as you hold a flower nail and cover with ruffles, using tube 103. Stick stem in styrofoam to dry.

Show off your flowers so they look their beautiful best

Flowers and leaves on stems
This method gives you the freedom to arrange flowers just like real ones. Pipe a mound of royal icing on a square of wax paper. Use the tube best suited to the weight of the flower—for the light weight nasturtium we used tube 4. Insert a length of florists' wire and brush the icing up on the wire to form calyx. Turn wire upright and stick in styrofoam to dry. Remove wax paper and attach dried flower to calyx with a dot of icing. By doing this in assembly-line fashion, you can stem many flowers in a short time.

To make stemmed leaves, pipe an anchoring dab on wax paper. Lay a piece of fine florists' wire on the dab, then pipe the leaf so that the center vein is directly over the wire. Dry. Bind with floral tape (see page 155).

Give flowers a lift
Marshmallows are very handy to mount flowers on. Remove the cornstarch coating with a clean damp cloth and secure to the cake top with a mound of icing. Pipe a mound of icing on the back of the dried flower and set it on the marshmallow, tilting it for the best effect. Conceal the marshmallow with more flowers and leaves. Use full-size or miniature marshmallows.

To attach flowers firmly on the side of a cake, pipe a royal icing spike on the back of the dried flower. Use any round tube, suiting it to the size of the flower. When the spike is thoroughly dry, pipe a little icing around it, and push the flower into the side of the cake.

Make fluffy cascades
Any lightweight blooms are suitable. Pipe a diamond-shaped zigzag on top edge of cake, extending down side. Pipe a second smaller zigzag on top of it, and press in flowers, first on edge, then filling in center. Finish with a few perky leaves.

Pose flowers on marshmallows for added height.

Pipe a spike on back of flower for cake side

50

1976. "Wilton Enterprises built a new headquarters in Woodridge, Illinois. I'm sure Dewey McKinley Wilton would be proud of the fine family of Wilton workers. I must say the people who really made all this possible are the millions of customers all over the world."—NORMAN WILTON

Cake serving and cutting charts

Serving and cutting chart for party cakes

The servings suggested below are dessert-sized portions of *two-layer cakes*, each layer about 2" high. If your cake, or cake tier is a single layer, cut the number of servings in half. Most one-mix cakes of any shape serve twelve.

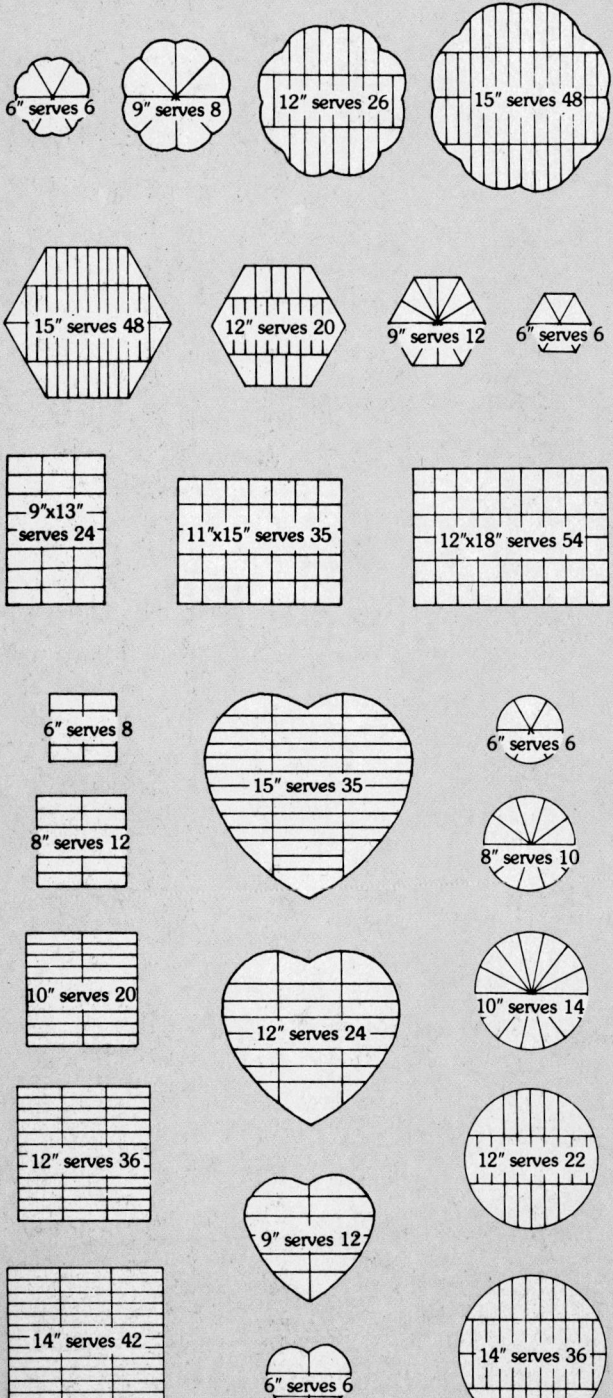

Serving chart for wedding and groom's cakes

Following the cutting charts below, here is a list of the number of servings you can expect from each cake tier. *Tiers are two-layer*, each tier 3" to 4" high. Individual servings are approximately 1" wide, 2" deep and two layers high. If the tier is one layer, cut the number of servings in half. Wedding cakes are traditionally cut in smaller slices than party cakes, but customs may vary in your community.

SHAPE	SIZE	SERVINGS	SHAPE	SIZE	SERVINGS
ROUND	6"	16	HEXAGON	6"	6
	8"	30		9"	22
	10"	48		12"	50
	12"	68		15"	66
	14"	92	PETAL	6"	8
	16"	118		9"	20
	18"	148		12"	44
SQUARE	6"	18		15"	62
	8"	32	HEART	6"	12
	10"	50		9"	28
	12"	72		12"	48
	14"	98		15"	90
	16"	128			
	18"	162			

How to cut a wedding or groom's cake

Begin by removing the top tier. Most brides freeze this for the first anniversary. Until you get to the base tier, remove each tier from the cake before cutting it. This is much easier and safer than attempting to cut the tiers while they are still part of the main cake. Cut groom's cakes the same way as wedding cakes.

How to cut a round tier

Make a circular cut 2" in from the tier edge, and cut 1" slices from it. Move in another 2", make a circular cut and slice that. Continue until the tier is completely cut. Cut the center core of each tier in quarters or sixths, depending on size.

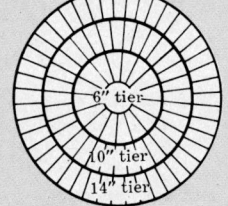

Top view of three-tiered round cake

How to cut a square tier

Move in 2" from the outer edge of the tier and make a cut, then cut 1" slices from it. Repeat until the entire tier is cut.

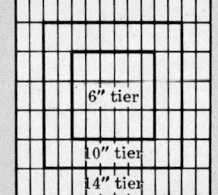

Top view of a three-tiered square cake

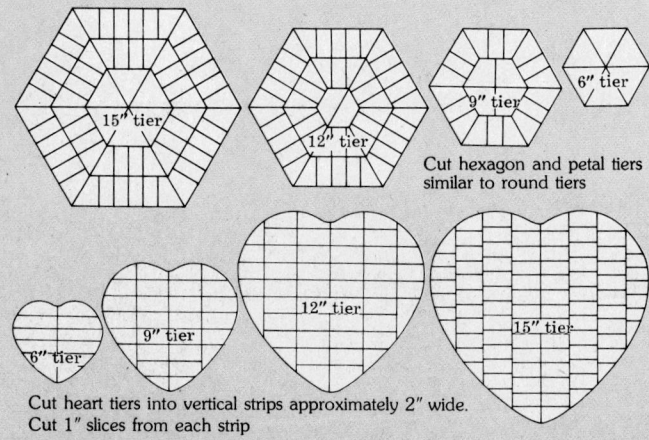

Cut hexagon and petal tiers similar to round tiers

Cut heart tiers into vertical strips approximately 2" wide. Cut 1" slices from each strip

Tested icing recipes

Wilton snow-white buttercream
A four-star icing—pure white, it covers well and pipes clear borders and flowers for cake top.

- ⅔ cup water
- 4 tablespoons Wilton Meringue Powder
- 1¼ cups solid white shortening, room temperature
- ¾ teaspoon salt
- ¼ teaspoon butter flavoring
- ½ teaspoon almond flavoring
- ½ teaspoon clear vanilla flavoring
- 11½ cups sifted confectioners' sugar

Combine water and meringue powder and whip at high speed until peaks form. Add four cups sugar, one cup at a time, beating after each addition at low speed. Alternately add shortening and remainder of sugar. Add salt and flavorings and beat at low speed until smooth. Thin with two teaspoons white corn syrup for leaves and strings. May be stored, well covered, in refrigerator for several weeks, then brought to room temperature and rebeaten. Yield: 8 cups.

Wilton chocolate buttercream
Easy to use, exceptionally good-tasting.

- ⅓ cup butter
- ⅓ cup solid white shortening
- ½ cup cocoa
- ½ cup milk
- 1 pound confectioners' sugar, sifted
- 5 tablespoons cool milk or cream
- 1 teaspoon vanilla
- ⅛ teaspoon salt

Cream butter and shortening together with an electric mixer. Mix cocoa and ½ cup milk and add to creamed mixture. Beat in sugar, one cup at a time, blending well after each addition and scraping sides and bottom of bowl frequently. Add cool milk, vanilla and salt and beat at high speed until light and fluffy. Keep icing covered with a lid or damp cloth and store in refrigerator. Bring to room temperature and rebeat. Stiffen with a little confectioners' sugar for cake top flowers. Do not thin for making leaves. Yield: 3⅔ cups.

Wilton boiled icing—meringue
Good for piping flowers and borders, but dries too crisp for covering the cake.

- 4 level tablespoons Wilton Meringue Powder
- 1 cup warm water
- 2 cups granulated sugar
- ¼ teaspoon cream of tartar
- 3½ cups sifted confectioners' sugar

Boil granulated sugar, ½ cup water and cream of tartar to 240°F. Brush side of pan with warm water to keep crystals from forming. Meanwhile, mix meringue powder with ½ cup water, beat 7 minutes at high speed. Turn to low speed, add confectioners' sugar, beat 4 minutes at high speed. Slowly add boiled sugar mixture, beat 5 minutes at high speed. Keeps a week in the refrigerator, covered with a damp cloth. Rebeat to use again. Yield: 6 cups. Use heavy-duty mixer for double recipe.

Wilton boiled icing—egg white
An excellent flavored icing for covering the cake. Do not use to pipe borders or flowers.

- 2 cups granulated sugar
- ½ cup water
- ¼ teaspoon cream of tartar
- 4 egg whites (room temperature)
- 1½ cups confectioners' sugar, measured then sifted

Boil granulated sugar, water and cream of tartar to 240°F. Brush sides of pan with warm water to prevent crystals. Brush again halfway through, but do not stir. Meanwhile, whip egg whites 7 minutes at high speed. Add boiled sugar mixture slowly, beat 3 minutes at high speed. Turn to second speed, gradually add confectioners' sugar, beat 7 minutes more at high speed. Rebeating won't restore texture. Yield: 3½ cups. Use heavy-duty mixer for double recipe.

Wilton royal icing—egg white
Use this durable, hard-drying icing for piping flowers, lace and fine stringwork.

- 3 egg whites (room temperature)
- 1 pound confectioners' sugar
- ½ teaspoon cream of tartar

Combine ingredients, beat at high speed 7 to 10 minutes. Dries quickly—keep covered. Rebeating will not restore. Yield: 3 cups.

Marzipan
- 1 cup almond paste (8 ounce can)
- 2 egg whites, unbeaten
- 3 cups confectioners' sugar
- ½ teaspoon vanilla or rum flavor

Knead almond paste by hand in a bowl. Add egg whites and mix well. Continue kneading as you add sugar, one cup at a time, and flavoring, until marzipan feels like heavy pie dough. Cover with plastic wrap, then place in a tightly covered container in the refrigerator to keep for months.

To tint, knead in a drop of liquid food color at a time until a natural shade is achieved.

To glaze marzipan pieces, combine ½ cup corn syrup and one cup water, heat to boiling and brush on. This gives a soft shine. For a high gloss, use just one or two tablespoons water with ½ cup corn syrup.

To put marzipan pieces together, brush one lightly with egg white, then fix to second with a turning motion.

Rolled fondant
This rolled icing gives a perfectly smooth decorating surface with a satiny finish.

- 2 pounds confectioners' sugar, sieved three times
- ½ ounce gelatin
- ¼ cup water
- ½ cup glucose
- ¾ ounce glycerine
- 2 or 3 drops clear flavoring
- liquid food color, as desired

Heat gelatin and water in a small pan until just dissolved. Put sieved sugar in a large bowl and make a depression in the center. Add glucose and glycerine to the dissolved gelatin and mix well. Pour mixture into depression in sugar and mix with your hands to a dough-like consistency. Transfer to a smooth surface lightly dusted with cornstarch and knead until smooth and pliable. Add flavoring and color while kneading. If too soft, knead in a little sieved confectioners' sugar. If too stiff, add a few drops of boiling water.

Use immediately or store in an airtight container at room temperature for up to a week. If storing longer, refrigerate and bring to room temperature before kneading and rolling out on work surface thinly coated with non-stick pan release and dusted with cornstarch. Recipe will cover an 8" x 3" square or a 9" x 3" round cake. See page 29 for how to cover the cake.

Wilton quick poured fondant
This icing for covering the cake dries to a smooth, shiny, grease-free finish.

- 6 cups confectioners' sugar
- 4½ ounces water
- 2 tablespoons corn syrup
- 1 teaspoon almond flavoring

Combine water and corn syrup. Add to sugar in a saucepan and stir over low heat until well-mixed, lukewarm and just thin enough to be poured. Stir in flavor and color.

To cover cake, ice thinly with buttercream. Place cake on cooling rack with a pan or cookie sheet beneath it. Pour fondant over iced cake, flowing from center and moving out in a circular motion. Excess fondant can be reheated and poured again. Yields four cups—covers an 8" cake.

Chocolate quick poured fondant
Follow recipe for Quick Poured Fondant, but increase amount of water by 1 ounce. After it is heated, stir in 3 ounces of melted, unsweetened chocolate, then add flavoring.

Stabilized whipped cream
- 1 teaspoon unflavored gelatin
- 2 tablespoons cold water
- 1 cup heavy whipping cream (at least 24 hours old and very cold)
- 2 tablespoons confectioners' sugar
- ½ teaspoon vanilla

Add gelatin to cold water in a small metal or pyrex cup. Set in a small pan of boiling water and heat until gelatin dissolves and looks clear (do not stir). Cool gelatin to room temperature. Make sure beaters and bowl are very cold, then whip cream to medium consistency. Pour dissolved gelatin into center all at once and continue beating. Also add confectioners' sugar and vanilla at this time. Beat only until cream stands in stiff peaks and clings to side of bowl. Yield: 2 cups.

happy years of decorating

Index

ANIMAL CAKES
  bird 66
  bunny 55, 61, 69
  butterfly 98, 139, 140
  cardinal 133
  chicken 139
  chicks 60, 66
  duck 60
  elephant 103
  fish 30, 140
  lamb 134
  lion 10, 134
  mice 102
  owl 92
  penguin 102
  reindeer 130
  seal 10
ANNIVERSARY CAKES
  1, 39, 95, 109, 120, 121, 122, 143
ANNOUNCEMENT CAKE 82
BABY SHOWER CAKES
  69, 139, 140, 141
BIRTHDAY CAKES
  1, 5-38, 138, 140, 141, 143, 144
BON VOYAGE CAKES
  50, 106
BORDERS 149-152
BRIDAL SHOWER CAKES
  64, 65, 70
CANDY
  cakes trimmed with 7, 9, 21, 22, 32, 40, 46, 131
  recipes 126, 128
CHILDREN'S CAKES
  6-19, 105, 124, 137, 138, 139, 143
  boys 16, 17, 18, 19, 105, 138, 143
  girls 12, 13, 14, 15, 105, 124, 143
  tots 6, 7, 9, 10, 139
CHOCOLATE, tempering 33
CHRISTMAS
  cakes 124, 129, 130, 131, 133, 134, 143, 144
  candy 126-128
  cookie village 123, 136
  decorations 123, 124, 125, 132, 136
COLOR FLOW
  17, 18, 24, 27, 31, 84, 98, 120, 133, 138, 142, 144
COMMONSENSE FOR DECORATORS 149-157
COOKIES
  cakes trimmed with 9, 18, 21, 36, 110, 114, 143
  decorated 112-113, 123, 124, 125, 129, 134
CUPCAKES
  10, 96, 111, 115
DECORATING FOR PROFIT
  145, 148
DECORATING TIPS
  144, 146-147
DOLL CAKES
  6, 14-15, 124
EASTER CAKES
  55, 60, 61, 66, 67
FATHER'S DAY CAKES
  86, 88, 90, 91

FIGURE PIPING
  10, 58, 59, 61, 66, 103, 124, 133, 138
FLOWERS, gum paste
  cakes trimmed with 56, 67, 79, 89
  California poppy 89, 94
  crocus 67
  impatiens 79
  lily 56
  tulip 56
FLOWERS, piped
  cakes trimmed with 5, 13, 21, 26, 32, 35, 36, 37, 39, 43, 45, 46, 47, 48, 49, 50, 53, 56, 60, 63, 65, 66, 71, 73, 74, 75, 78, 81, 82, 83, 84, 86, 87, 93, 95, 98, 99, 101, 103, 106, 109, 116, 117, 118, 121, 122, 137, 140, 144
  how to pipe 34, 42, 50, 57, 62, 82, 85, 116, 121, 153, 154, 155, 156
  mounting on wire stems 157
  bachelor buttons 26
  bluebonnet 155
  carnation 84, 156
  cherry blossom 116, 117
  chrysanthemum 109
  clover 106, 155
  daffodil 56, 87
  daisy 35, 75, 87, 95, 98, 140
  drop flowers 44, 46, 47, 49, 60, 65, 66, 78, 99, 101, 106
  forget-me-nots 48, 82, 83
  Golden Jubilee roses 73, 93, 122, 153
  goldenrod 106, 154
  hibiscus 50
  holly 133, 143
  iris 116, 117
  lilac 63, 154
  lily 5, 82, 83
  lily of the valley 63
  marigold 35
  morning glory 35, 153
  nasturtium 121
  pansy 86, 156
  petunia 81, 84, 137
  poinsettia 144
  quick rosebud 43
  rose 5, 37, 39, 48, 74, 82, 83, 87
  rose, Golden Jubilee 73, 93, 122, 153
  rosebud 45, 48, 118
  sego lily 155
  shaggy mum 116, 117
  sweet pea 43, 53, 71, 122
  tulip 43, 66
  violet 63, 156
FONDANT, recipes 159
  poured, cakes covered with 14, 49, 55, 60, 63, 73, 84, 90, 99, 101, 118
  rolled, cakes covered with 5, 71, 74, 75, 84, 121
FOURTH OF JULY CAKES
  98, 99
FRUIT, cakes trimmed with
  40, 41, 50, 111, 119

GINGERBREAD
  cakes trimmed with 18, 110, 134
  decorations 124, 125
  recipe 19
GRADUATION CAKES
  92, 93
GROOM'S CAKE 73
GUM PASTE
  Baroque molds 53, 100, 137
  cakes trimmed with 12, 25, 39, 54, 67, 79, 89, 104, 105, 137, 138
  figures 12, 39, 54, 89, 104, 105
  flowers 56, 67, 79, 89, 94
  records 25
  ship 138
  treasure box 100
  wreath 132
HALLOWEEN CAKES
  114, 115, 140
HISTORY OF WILTON ENTERPRISES
  62, 72, 96, 107, 108, 113, 126, 133, 135, 136, 157
HOBBY CAKES 25, 26, 27, 30, 31, 36, 88, 138, 139, 140, 144
ICING RECIPES 159
LACEWORK 39, 78
LATTICE
  43, 87, 95, 139, 140, 141
LEAVES, mounting on wire 157
MARZIPAN
  cakes trimmed with 30, 41, 51, 88, 90, 102, 119
  recipe 159
MEN'S CAKES
  26, 27, 28, 30, 31, 32, 38, 86, 88, 90, 91, 104, 138, 142, 143, 144
MOTHER'S DAY CAKES
  84, 87, 89
MOUNTING FLOWERS on wire stems 157
NEW YEAR'S CAKES
  52, 53
"NIFTY FIFTY" DECORATING TIPS
  146-147
PETITS FOURS
  14, 63
PIPING GEL
  27, 60, 66, 131, 141, 144
PULLED SUGAR
  1, 144
QUICK & CLEVER CAKES
  6, 7, 10, 13, 16, 18, 21, 22, 23, 26, 28, 32, 36, 38, 40, 41, 43, 44, 46, 47, 49, 60, 64, 65, 66, 69, 70, 91, 96, 99, 101, 106, 111, 114, 115, 117, 118, 128, 129, 130, 131, 134
READERS'
  cakes 137-144
  decorating for profit 145, 148
  "nifty fifty" decorating tips 146-147
RECIPES
  candy 126, 128

  gelatin candy 128
  gingerbread 19
  gum paste 13
  icings 159
  roll-out cookie dough 8
  sugar mold 11
"RIGHT ON THE CAKE" TECHNIQUES
  10, 13, 21, 24, 27, 28, 32, 36, 38, 40, 43, 46, 49, 52, 63, 66, 68, 70, 91, 96, 103, 106, 111, 114, 116-117, 118, 131, 137, 139, 140, 141, 143
ST. PATRICK'S DAY CAKES
  59, 62
SCHOOL TREATS
  96, 110, 111, 112-113
SESAME STREET CHARACTERS 9
SHEET CAKES
  7, 10, 21, 22, 25, 26, 27, 28, 32, 36, 38, 39, 40, 43, 49, 51, 64, 69, 70, 92, 93, 96, 106, 111, 114, 117, 124, 134, 137, 139, 140, 141, 142, 143, 144
SHOWER CAKES
  baby 69, 139, 140, 141
  bridal 64, 65, 70
SPACE CAKES
  22, 23
SPORTS CAKES
  24, 31, 38, 51, 104, 105, 142, 143
STAR METHOD
  6, 7, 14, 18, 32, 62, 64, 69, 99, 102, 103, 114, 115, 134, 137, 142
STEMS, mounting flowers on 157
SUGAR MOLD, cakes trimmed with 10, 36, 60, 69, 140
SWEETEST DAY CAKE 118
TEENAGE CAKES
  21, 22, 23, 24, 25, 26, 27, 138
THANK YOU GIFTS
  100, 101
THANKSGIVING CAKES
  119, 142
TIER CAKES
  9, 10, 17, 25, 28, 35, 39, 52, 53, 65, 66, 71, 73, 74, 75, 78, 79, 81, 83, 91, 93, 95, 98, 106, 109, 119, 120, 122
TOY CAKES
  6, 7, 10, 14-15, 69, 124, 139
USE OF SHAPED PANS
  6, 14-15, 16, 21, 22, 23, 32, 39, 41, 44, 46, 49, 50, 55, 60, 64, 90, 92, 93, 99, 101, 102, 106, 114, 115, 121, 124, 129, 131, 134
USES OF TUBES
  149-157
VALENTINE'S DAY
  39, 44, 45, 46, 47, 48, 49
WEDDING CAKES
  39, 71, 73, 74, 75, 78, 79, 81, 83, 95, 122
WOMEN'S CAKES
  35, 36, 37, 38, 84, 87, 89